IF YOU TEACH IT, THEY WILL READ

TOURO COLLEGE LIBRARY
Kings Hwy

Literature's Life Lessons for Today's Students

John V. MacLean

ROWMAN & LITTLEFIELD EDUCATION
A division of
ROWMAN & LITTLEFIELD PUBLISHERS, INC.
Lanham • New York • Toronto • Plymouth, UK

KH

Published by Rowman & Littlefield Education
A division of Rowman & Littlefield Publishers, Inc.
A wholly owned subsidiary of The Rowman & Littlefield Publishing Group, Inc.
4501 Forbes Boulevard, Suite 200, Lanham, Maryland 20706
http://www.rowmaneducation.com

Estover Road, Plymouth PL6 7PY, United Kingdom

British Library Cataloguing in Publication Information Available

Library of Congress Cataloging-in-Publication Data

MacLean, John V.
  If you teach it, they will read: literature's life lessons for today's students / John
V. MacLean.
        p. cm.
  Includes bibliographical references.
  ISBN 978-1-60709-777-8 (cloth : alk. paper) — ISBN 978-1-60709-778-5
(pbk. : alk. paper) — ISBN 978-1-60709-779-2
  1. Language arts (Secondary). 2. Reading (Secondary). 3. English language—
Composition and exercises—Study and teaching (Secondary). I. Title.
  LB1528.M283 2010
  807.1'273—dc22   2010013969

Printed in the United States of America.

9/2/11

This book is dedicated to my wife, Mary,
to my children, Cora, Caitlin, Emma, and Sarah,
and to three decades of high school students at
Burke Catholic and Woodlands High School.

* * *

Additional thanks go to Thomas Koerner of Rowman & Littlefield,
and to Tony Howarth, Carol Harrington, and Ron Ross
for their careful reading of and valued comments
on the manuscript.

Introduction
Why Read Good Books?

SOME YEARS AGO, I complained to my daughter's high school principal that the curriculum for her ninth-grade combined English–social studies course required students to read only two books in an entire year. The principal responded that she would not sacrifice quality for quantity and that she would not "add any book to the curriculum unless it can be made part of a meaningful educational activity."

The quote is exact, because I went straight home and wrote it down. The message was clear. Reading novels or plays and discussing their ideas or the beauty and precision of their expression did not constitute a meaningful educational activity in my daughter's highly rated public high school.

Over the years, I have mentored a number of student teachers, graduate students earning their MS in education. When I offer them a book to teach to the class, the first response of the most diligent is, "I'll try to think of some activities." I always suggest that they start by considering what the book is about, why the author wrote it, and what ideas the students might find important.

Teaching literature is in trouble, and the premise of this book is that the fault is not with illiterate students. On the contrary, my experience has been that students are willing, able, and even eager to discuss ideas and to read books (even long ones) for what they have to say. Students can even be made to see that books offer them a way to deal with the universal fears that beset each one of them in his or her heart of hearts. In other words, even teenagers can find comfort in books.

Teenagers are not afraid of real literature—educators are. If this is a "how to" book, it is about how not to be afraid of real books. It is about how not to be afraid of challenging a seventeen-year-old with a two-thousand-year-old idea. It's about how to help that seventeen-year-old make that idea his or her own. This book will offer neither scholarly disputations of the literature discussed nor a primer on how to teach. What it will offer is a discussion of books from the perspective of ideas that I have found to resonate with young people.

I have limited this book to a discussion of the books I actually teach, in a public school noted for its ethnic, economic, and intellectual diversity. I have limited the discussion to the ideas my students and I have discussed and the life lessons we have learned from this literature.

While these young people may seem adrift in an MTV world— posturing nonchalance and wallowing in materialism—they are rightfully scared to death of a world they have inherited from us, a world where bad things happen to good people, where individuals find it ever more difficult to make a mark, where problems have spiraled out of control, where existence seems both pointless and tenuous, and where God is dead or ordering us to hate one another. It is also a world where fantasy offers a needed escape from information overload and reality television. Did any generation ever have a more acute need for literature?

As I write this, my ten-year-old is halfway through the last nine-hundred-page Harry Potter novel. In the remaining eight years before she heads for college, how often will she be encouraged, let alone required, to find a meaningful experience in a nine-hundred-page read? How often will curriculum designers assume that anything longer than 150 pages will send her scurrying to Cliffs Notes or Pinkmonkey. com? How often will they assume that a child who can devour the saga of life at Hogwarts will be unable to find relevance in the life of Huck Finn or Odysseus? How often will they assume that her quiet engagement with a book is inadequate evidence of mental activity?

The sorry truth is that the study of literature is becoming marginalized in the high school curriculum, and even in introductory college classes. There are several reasons for this.

The first problem is that your typical high school English teacher must spend more time teaching literacy than literature and must do so, not by helping students love books, but by teaching to standardized tests. Students who do not succeed with the tests face endless rounds of remediation. One might argue that if students were taught consistently that reading books is something worth doing, then they would read more and need less remediation. However, any teacher of "elective" courses, from technology to band, will tell you that state requirements for test performance levels are putting a squeeze on other student activities.

Unfortunately, in the English class, literature has been relegated too often to the status of an elective. There is less time to discuss novels, plays, and poems when there is so much test practice to be done. There is certainly nothing ignoble about teaching literacy, and there is nothing wrong with a public demanding that its high schools and colleges produce young people who can function in today's economy. However, part of one's ability to function depends just as much on the lessons of literature.

Books offer us ways to deal with dark nights of the soul; they offer us philosophical and moral underpinnings for daily life, and they offer us a connection with human aspiration that extends from Homer to Toni Morrison. In the greater or even lesser scheme of things, surely this is as important as one's ability to fill out a job application or write a business letter.

On the first day of class with my seniors, I pass around a Greek coin dating from the reign of Alexander the Great. (Yes, most of them have heard of him. Remember, this is a book about what students *can* do.) I ask them if they can think of why I would be starting class this way, and questioning eventually gets someone around to the right answer.

When they touch the coin, they connect with every human being who ever touched it—including the other human beings in their classroom. The coin might have been in Alexander's toga pocket. More likely, some average Alex used it to buy a pair of sandals or a jug of wine. However, the people who held it over two thousand years ago were people like us, who asked the same questions we do, who wanted the same things for themselves and their families. We touch them when we touch the coin, and we touch them when we touch *The Odyssey*, a book that was already ancient literature, even for them.

One of the hardest things about adolescence is the young person's sense that he or she is alone. Each one is convinced that nobody has ever been so brokenhearted, faced such bitter disappointments, yearned more to establish an identity, felt more insecure. When you see the gangs and cliques in our high schools and all you see is menace or superficiality, take another look.

I remind my students during that first class of a line from the film version of the play *Shadowlands*, based on the life of author C. S. Lewis: "We read to know we are not alone."[1] We can find in books the comfort of recognition, of shared pain and doubt and hope. What better way to function in today's world—in the workplace, the town meeting, the family—than to know that one is not alone, to know what one has in common with one's fellow human beings?

A second problem with teaching literature is the emphasis on "active learning." A class should be a series of activities and the teacher should be a coach, not an instructor. There is nothing wrong with this in theory, but the practice can result in classes where the activity is more prized than the learning.

I once saw a demonstration lesson, a well-constructed series of activities based on (if memory serves) Siegfried Sassoon's World War I poem, "Dreamers," where the majority of group discussion focused on how evidence in the poem would offer an unfamiliar reader an indication of which war the poet had experienced. The lesson was judged a success, because almost all students had something to say, and a supervisor duly noted exactly how many students spoke. The "bottom line"—never to be confused with the "least common denominator"—is that talking about nothing is better than thinking about something.

Of course, the brighter students were often rolling their eyes and making frustrated comments to their less able classmates such as, "Dugouts? Trenches? Can't you see it's World War I?"

The real problem was that they never said anything about the poem. They also never said anything that would touch them where they live—all of them, the most able and the least able. They did not talk about the pain and fear of young men going off to war. They did not talk about the nobility of sacrifice, the longing for home, the shattering of illusions.

I can't help think of the poor poet, watching his friends' lives ended on the Western Front when he himself was only a couple of years older than these students. In what he might have thought were his last weeks on earth, he had had something he wanted to tell my students—almost a dying declaration. I think the students would have been willing to listen, particularly given the fact that many of them had friends or relatives serving in Afghanistan and Iraq.

What if Sassoon had known, writing from the experience of his rat-infested dugout, that his poem about the dreams of doomed youth would be reduced to a scavenger hunt (Alliteration—"flaming, fatal climax"; Rhyme—"tomorrows . . . sorrows"), that the deepest thoughts it would be allowed to inspire were a search for evidence of which war his friends were dying in rather than what thoughts their dying inspired? Like his German comrade in *All Quiet on the Western Front*, he might have died in peace and blessed the sniper.

While it is true that too much traditional teaching is based on the teacher's unwillingness to trust his or her students and let them go on their own, it is also true that much of active learning is based on an unwillingness to trust the students and let them sit and think, without the comforting cacophony of voices, without even putting them in groups.

The push for active learning can lead to novels becoming mere grist for the activity mill. Teach *The Scarlet Letter*, not because teenagers might really be interested in sin and redemption, but because students might actually be confronting in their own lives the distinctions between wrongs committed against society, against morality, and against "the human heart." Teach the book because it's Thanksgiving, the social studies class has reached the Pilgrims, and the home economics class is baking squash.

In recent years, English teachers who came to the profession with a master's degree in literature have had to adapt their methods to new understandings of cognitive learning styles and to new expectations about skills uniformly assessed. The new generation of English teachers, armed with master's of science in English education, may likewise have to adapt to students now inactively reading Harry Potter without a thought to improving their SAT vocabulary skills or engaging in a group project to build models of Hogwarts.

So, here's the kind of simple activity I do before *The Odyssey*. It will not necessarily improve their SAT scores, but it might just make more accessible one of the greatest works of literature the world has ever known. It may also help them think a bit about their own lives.

One problem students have with Homer is that once you get beyond the cartoon stories of Greek mythology, it's just too ridiculous to think of people who believed that river gods, tree gods, fluorescent light gods could actually play around with people's fate. How can we take such ideas seriously? What can they possibly say to us? More than ever, we determine our own lives—don't we? I set my students a simple task. (Our classes must begin with a do-now, an immediate activity to start class.) I ask the students, starting with their birth, to make a list of all the facts about them that conspired to put them in their seats this morning. Then we have some fun.

I ask them when they were floating around in the ether, did they decide to be born to those two people in New York, rather than those two down there in Sarajevo, or those two in Rwanda? Might they have arrived at their teenage years with some different attitudes, concerns, options had they been born in the middle of a war zone? Was that their choice, any more than it was for the children of Sarajevo or Rwanda? Did they decide to be born female, black, intelligent, athletic, wealthy? How much of their self-confidence comes from their good looks? Was that just a good choice on their part?

What happened next? If their parents moved, did they ask for the students' opinion? Has moving made it easier for them to find lasting friendships? Did they decide whether a parent would lose a job? Has the state of their parents' marriage had any effect on their success in school? This is fate. Surely, nurture and good hard work can make a difference—but only up to a point, only within the parameters set by fate. By the time we hit high school, we've all been dealt different cards.

So what do we do? Is life only about fate? Do our decisions matter at all? Certainly, every high school and college is full of kids who can never get beyond the unfairness of it all. As Shakespeare says, "When in disgrace with fortune and men's eyes," they curse their fate, wishing themselves like to one more rich in hope, featured like him, like him with friends possessed. Like Shakespeare in his sonnet, they dream away their identities: if only I could be a singer or sports star, or at least be on the *Real World* or *Road Rules*, where my every puerile utterance could be imbued with significance.

Why shouldn't our high schools be full of such people, when our adult society is full of them? If you hit yourself in the head with an ax that didn't have a warning label telling you not to use it to cut hair, call 1-800 Sue Them. If you murder someone, say it was the sugar in the Twinkies that made you do it. Ultimately would-be adults have to get beyond the child's mantra of "it's not fair," to the more mature "you have to deal with it." Isn't that still what courage is all about? We deal with our fate; we make the most of it.

Don't whine. Hemingway said so. Don't try to be somebody you were never born to be, but make sure you make the best of what you are. The ancient Greeks said so.

The kids get it, and they arrive at the conclusions on their own, even if not every one of them says something, nobody falls asleep, even at 8:00 in the morning.

A wonderful poem to include in a consideration of fate and its implications is Robert Frost's "Design."[2] The poem is a sonnet. The first four lines set the scene—Frost's discovery of a moth in the clutches of a spider. The next four lines make additional, disturbing observations, and the poem turns in line nine toward the questions—why was the flower white instead of its usual blue, why was the spider white, how did it know to climb that flower, why did the moth choose to land on it? The diction stresses the innocence of the spider. It is white and dimpled, and holds the moth like a kite. The tone shifts from the gruesome invocation of a witches' brew right out of Macbeth, to a breakfast cereal jingle, "mixed ready to begin the morning right."

In a thoroughly designed, fated world, nothing is guilty. Therefore, nothing is innocent. What was to blame? "What but design of darkness to appall? If design govern in a thing so small."

The implication is clear. If design governs there, it governs in our larger portion of the universe as well. The fact that the poem is in sonnet form—the most "designed" verse form in English— underscores the point. But the larger point is still what we will do with the inescapable fact that larger forces sometimes shape our ends, as much as we Americans like to champion our individual efforts.

Now, what about all of Homer's gods? Ask the following questions: What about the accident that ruined your new car? What about the stomach virus that ruined your chance to make sectional champion? Why did one person get caught cheating on a test, when everyone in class knows it was the first time he ever did it and the kid in the next row has been getting away with it all year? Why did your best friend have to move? Why did your grandmother have to get sick? Such events can go beyond just being dismissed as bad luck. They hurt too much, and leave us looking—often angrily—for answers.

As the Anglo-Saxon poet of "The Wanderer" says, "Fate's will changeth the world / Wealth is lent us, friends are lent us / man is lent, kin is lent."[3]

When a Greek baby drowned and his grieving parents blamed the angry river god, they were looking for answers. They also asked themselves if there was something they might have done to propitiate the god to keep calamity at bay. Ultimately, weren't they just acknowledging that life is fickle, and painfully so, and that tragedies happen that we humans would like to explain with some rule of logic, but about which we have no clue?

Not much action here, but lots to think about. Actively debating minutiae may serve to hone some interpersonal skills, but the function of literature, and at least one of the functions of education, is to give our future citizens some way of framing ultimate questions. This is the ultimate problem with the mind-numbing utilitarianism of modern American education.

Scientists are increasingly alarmed that a dearth of pure research in our universities—of time and money devoted to pursuits with no immediate patentable return—will stifle creativity in the future. The pure research of literature is the search for connection with our fellow human beings. If we abandon it for activities that provide incremental improvements in language arts assessment, what effect will this have on our future?

As another principal told me recently, "You can't get a diploma in theater." How can we waste time, and money, on Wilde or Wilson when there is so much test material to be covered and so much remediation to be done? If we have to do "literature," make sure we limit our students to short, ruthlessly topical "problem" novels like Amy and Her Abortion or Barbie and Her Bulimia. We can throw in a few magazine articles and have the kids write a nice practice essay for their ELA competency test.[4]

Famous high school failure Albert Einstein said that real education could begin only when we forgot everything we had been forced to learn in high school. And remember what Paul Simon told us about the "crap" he had learned.

Writing of Mr. Summler's Planet, Stanley Crouch says: "What protects the world from the eradication of its humanity is the willingness to empathize with the range of mortal triumph, mortal folly, and mortal pain. The transcendent willingness allows us to say, even to the dead, 'we know, we know, we know.'"[5]

To turn away from literature is to turn away from education's greatest lessons, the appreciation of our shared humanity, the unflinching apprehension of the human condition.[6]

The true irony of all this is that high school and college students are poised at a unique moment in their lives, when they first prepare to leave the nest, to make decisions. As the next chapter on rite of passage will discuss, they are dying to understand this juncture they've reached and terrified, beneath all the anger and bravado, by what comes next. They need the reassurance that others have been there before. Some of those others even wrote it down.

NOTES

1. William Nicholson, *Shadowlands* (screenplay based on his play). Price Entertainment/Spelling Films International.

2. Robert Frost, "Design," in Edward Conneery Lathem (ed.), *The Poetry of Robert Frost*. New York: Henry Holt, 1969.

3. "The Wanderer," in Michael Alexander (trans.), *The Earliest English Poems*. London: Penguin, 1969.

4. Obviously, I do not mean to minimize the importance of such issues, only the literary value of novels whose primary purpose is to illustrate them. To see literature arranged around "teen issues" in an effective way, see Neil Astley's poetry anthology *Staying Alive*, published by Bloodaxe Books.

5. Sidney Crouch (introduction) in Saul Bellow's *Mr. Sammler's Planet*. New York: Penguin Twentieth Century Classics, 2004.

6. English was not even studied in England before 1828, and in 1887 history professor Edward Freeman successfully fought the teaching of literature at Oxford, stating, "We are told that the study of literature 'cultivates the taste education and sympathies and enlarges the mind.' These are excellent things, only we cannot examine tastes and sympathies. Examiners must have technical and positive information to examine." The needs of examiners trumped the need for enlarged minds at Oxford for the next seven years and, even when an English course was offered, it was heavily weighted with language study. As Freeman added, "what is meant by distinguishing literature from language if by literature is meant the study of great books and not mere chatter about Shelley?" See Peter Barry's *Beginning Theory: An Introduction to Literary and Cultural Theory*. Manchester, UK: Manchester University Press, 2009, 12–14.

Chapter One

The Search for Identity

Cyrano de Bergerac and
A Lesson before Dying

What does it mean to "be your own person"?
How do relationships with others define me?

"WHO'S THERE?" IS THE OPENING LINE of *Hamlet*. What a great opening line for a course of literature inviting students to use their study to study themselves. As Shakespeare says in his sonnet (ii):

> When in disgrace with fortune and men's eyes,
> I all alone and weep my outcast fate,
> And trouble deaf heaven with my bootless cries,
> And look upon myself and curse my fate.[1]

What student has not been here? All alone, an outcast. As President Barack Obama himself said in his September 2009 speech to the nation's schoolchildren, "There were times when I was lonely and felt like I didn't fit in."[2] Students may not know what "bootless" means. (The word "boot," as a thing worn on the foot, comes from Old French. The Old English word means good, or of worth. It gives us the expression "to boot," and—say it if you dare to high school students—"booty.") But they certainly know the feeling that nobody, not even God, is listening.

What they typically do in this situation is exactly the wrong thing. They feel their problems would be solved "if only." If only they could play basketball like him, or be as clever as someone else,

1

all would be well. It's a short step from wanting to be like someone else, to wanting to be someone else instead of who you are. You forget what you yourself have, can, and might yet do.

> Wishing me like to one more rich in hope,
> Featured like him, like him with friends possessed,
> Desiring this man's art and that man's scope,
> With what I most enjoy contented least

Thank goodness, we're at line 9 and the "turn."

> Yet in these thoughts, myself almost despising—
> Haply I think on thee: and then my state,
> Like to the Lark at break of day arising
> From sullen earth, sings hymns at Heaven's gate

Remind students that they are not alone—not really. Remembering that there have been, in the course of their young lives, some people who liked them, who may not have liked them if they had been like someone else is enough to keep them from really despising themselves.

> For thy sweet love rememb'red such wealth brings
> That then I scorn to change my state with Kings

Point out to students that not even a king of England could have such friends, because "they don't know him the way they know me." This starts them thinking maybe they are worth knowing after all. What could be a more critical lesson for any high school student?

One of literature's famous outcasts, who learns too late the power of one person's love, is Cyrano de Bergerac.[3] The play was written two centuries after the glory days in which it is set. One wonders if Rostand saw it as a needed prescription for his own, more modern France. One wonders if it could help our even more modern America, with its lessons about overcoming mere vanity with true values and the nobility of the individual spirit.

Cyrano himself is vain, too defensive about his nose to countenance the possibility that mere goodness could win love. For a time, his lovely Roxane matches the same vice, as she demands of the honest but tongue-tied Christian that he rhapsodize in order to win her. She is not content with the three words some wait their entire lives to hear—"I love you." In the death scene, Cyrano fights all his old enemies, and Vanity is the last.

Granted, Cyrano dies, but what a life he leads. The insult scene, where he shows a fool how to insult with wit his giant nose, is wonderful, even when all you can show is the grainy but Academy Award–winning Jose Ferrer version. When you also show the Steve Martin version from *Roxanne*,[4] the scene gives rise to a great writing assignment.

Have the students pick a feature of themselves about which they are sensitive—but not too sensitive. Hair, nose, feet (a real favorite), and rear ends seem to predominate. Ask them then to compose a list of twenty insults (beware of the presence on the Internet of "fat jokes," etc.) and receive extra credit for delivering them with appropriate gusto in front of the class. (After the first two do theirs, everyone wants a go.)

To glory in who an individual is, complete with what the style magazines would see as flaws, is the epitome of mental health. We don't need to wish life away wishing we were someone else.

A second writing assignment comes from Cyrano's "No thank you" speech. Having been rebuffed by Roxane, Cyrano sacrifices his own feelings for hers. The villain De Guiche then makes him an offer he finds he can refuse. When his best friend asks why he insists on being so independent, he replies, "What would you have me do?" He then lists a series of servile actions that he will not undertake, even for financial gain or popularity, and follows this with a list of those things that give him joy—even if they mean standing alone.

In a high school classroom rife with peer pressure, I encourage students to make their own poetic manifesto about what they won't do and what they demand the right to do. Again, extra credit is given for the best, and perhaps a spot in the school newspaper's editorial page for delivering them aloud.

The balcony scene, in which Christian makes a fool of himself and is rescued by Cyrano, who wins his love for someone else, serves to raise real moral questions of self-sacrifice and love. Again, the parallel scene from *Roxanne* is great fun. However, as Cyrano reminds Roxane, and himself:

> Love hates that game of words! It is a crime to fence with life—I tell you there comes one moment, once—and God help those who pass that moment by!—when Beauty stands looking into the soul with grave, sweet eyes that sicken at petty words.

Real human emotions require real, honest response. We are back to the courtly romance of the Arthurian legends, but also touching the universal that students can appreciate.

Cyrano defines himself largely in opposition to his society. Again, the indictment of a valueless society seems to be part of the work. However, humans are social beings, and we also define ourselves through our interactions with others. Louis Gaines's *A Lesson before Dying*[5] also deals with a very particular society where subtle differences loom large. This world is even closer to the world of our students.

The novel presents a vivid portrait of a pre-*Brown v. Board of Education*, "separate but equal," schoolroom and all-too-familiar distinctions between black and white. However, it also shows more subtle divisions within the black community: light and dark, educated and uneducated, religious and irreligious. Like the works of Jane Austen, the novel also shows how the little things in life, often subtle awareness of language and gesture, are what make a man a man, a woman a woman—a person a person. Like Austen's work, Gaines's novel is firmly rooted in the specifics of a vividly recalled world, but it, too, touches the universal.

The novel begins with a young black man caught in the wrong place at the wrong time and condemned for the murder of a white man. Jefferson's lawyer is no Atticus Finch. He's the dark side of Bigger Thomas's Mr. Max. He argues that Jefferson should receive leniency not because he is a helpless victim, but because he is a lower life-form. He is "a hog." The local schoolteacher, Grant Wiggins, is reluctantly impressed by his aunt into the job of teaching Jefferson that he is not a hog, but a man. This is a lesson we all need to learn before dying.

As Albert Camus reminds us, we are all under a sentence of death.[6] Before our time comes, and it could come at any time, we had better be sure that we can look in the mirror and see a human being and not a hog. Our society is good at producing hogs, as surely as Circe could with her seductive magic. If the "no, you can't" of racism cannot do it, the "why not" of permissive consumerism can. In Jefferson's case, it is not laziness or selfishness that keeps him sullen and unresponsive to his godmother and to her emissary; it is a very justifiable anger that has little outlet.

Few of us are treated with the injustice that crushes Jefferson, but all of us live with the awareness that life will end, and that our goodness will not extend it one moment. The educated Wiggins is separated by many things from the community in which he grew up and in which he continues to work. One of the most important is his inability to accept the community's religious fervor. With no belief in an afterlife, he is hard pressed to offer solace to Jefferson and comes into conflict with the local pastor, who wants above all for Jefferson to accept salvation as his lesson before dying.

Wiggins must wrestle with his own beliefs, not only about religion but also about his purpose in working in his substandard school in a world that seems not to change for all his effort, about his connection to a land that offers the memory of slavery along with the solace of community, about his responsibility to a woman that has to go beyond sex, about his place in a universe he sees as amoral and uncaring. Wiggins's aunt insists he undertake the challenge of reaching Jefferson. His own girlfriend insists as well. They do so as much for Wiggins as for Jefferson. We all need to learn the lesson before dying.

The endless series of petty indignities heaped upon Wiggins by the white society is beautifully expressed, but more important and just as subtle are the frustrations he feels with himself. His own former teacher is a model of the frustrated idealist who has become a cynic, true to Wilde's definition of a man who knows the price of everything and the value of nothing. He has seen the cost to himself of a life spent working in the Jim Crow South. However, he can see no value in his efforts, no value in education, which seems powerless to effect change.

As the old saying goes, if you are not a liberator, you are an oppressor, and Wiggins, like his own dying teacher, is in danger of becoming no more than a part of the oppressive system.

The lesson that Wiggins learns along with Jefferson is that many of the most oppressive facts of our lives, including the fact that our lives must end, cannot be changed. However, the heroic need not be herculean. To prove we are humans and not hogs, we must accept our fate as the Greeks did, but at the same time refuse to accept any diminution in our humanity.

The small kindness, the sacrifice for others who would likewise sacrifice for us, the breaking of bread, the acceptance of community—it is these things as much as our brainpower that assure us of our sense of worth. Jefferson's newfound sense of purpose and his quiet strength in the face of death allow his dying to bring a community together, to reassure Wiggins of his place in it, and even to nudge a white deputy into what might be the possibility for a better world.

The question of what we are willing to do for others largely determines our ability to establish who we are, and this is just as important as the question of what we will not do at the behest of others. All too often our teenagers define themselves by their popularity, by what they feel they must do to earn acceptance. It is acceptance of others, not by others, that shows us our humanity. It is the things we do for others that earn us the reward, but only if we don't seek that reward in the first place.

Students are struggling to find out who they are in a world all too ready to give them all the wrong answers. They are, ready or not, about to embark on a rite of passage. Are we ready to help them?

NOTES

1. William Shakespeare, "Sonnet (ii)," in Arthur Quiller-Couch (ed.), *The Oxford Book of English Verse 1250–1918*. New York: Oxford University Press, 1955.

2. Barack Obama, "Prepared Remarks of President Obama: Back to School Event, Arlington, Virginia." September 8, 2009. Retrieved from http://www.whitehouse.gov/mediaresources/PreparedSchoolRemarks/.

3. Edmund Rostand, *Cyrano de Bergerac* (Brian Hooker, trans.). New York: Bantam, 1981.

4. *Roxanne*, RCA/Columbia Pictures, 1987.

5. Ernest J. Gaines, *A Lesson before Dying*. New York: Vintage Contemporaries, 1993.

6. Albert Camus, "We should sentence no one to death since we have been sentenced to death ourselves." From "Notes on the Composition of *The Plague*," in *Selected Essays and Notebooks*. London: Penguin Peregrine Books, 1970.

Chapter Two

———○———

Rite of Passage

The Odyssey, The Adventures of
Huckleberry Finn, and Heart of Darkness

What happens when we leave the nest?
What happens when we confront the new and different?
Are we ready to make choices without the influence of parents,
    teachers, childhood friends?
What do we learn from these experiences?
What if we choose poorly?

THE RITE OF PASSAGE is a natural place to begin for high school students looking at their first real life choices. With sophomores now
taking college boards and being told of the need to develop résumés
and portfolios, students are being forced to consider what will become their first steps away from home. They may sit at computer
screens looking at sneaker ads and prom limo services, but they are
thinking of this nonetheless—and they are scared.

To add to their anxiety, we read "The Road Not Taken," and
I draw a line leading to a juncture—two roads converging in a
wood—and draw lines emerging from one of those lines. The college choice often leads to the place one finds a mate, a first job, a
circle of lifelong friends. The lines go on forever, but they look like
only half a tree. That road not taken lopped off the other half with
all its possibilities. An alternative life can be mapped out from that
turning: a different college, a different part of the country, different

spouse, friends, career, and so forth. Choose one and the other vanishes. Which one is right? Choice is scary.

The point of the rite of passage, however, is that choice is inevitable and that choice makes character. One must undertake the journey. As frightening as change may be, all I have to do is ask my students to think of people they know who never leave home after high school, who never leave town. We read Updike's "Ex-Basketball Player,"[1] and the students all know people who never got beyond high school, physically or emotionally.

Yes, I also point out all the poetic techniques—meter, end-stopped and non-end-stopped lines, diction, image, caesura—and even use the poem for a fill-in-the-blanks introductory paragraph for a literary essay.

> The poem "Ex Basketball Player," by John Updike, is about
> _____. The description in the first verse
> prepares us for Flick's story by _____. The
> street that "runs" past the high school lot is called Pearl Avenue
> because _____. The end-stop in line two
> has the effect of _____. This is further emphasized by the use of iambic pentameter in the next line,
> which underscores the idea of _____.
> The use of caesura in the next line offers a juxtaposition of Colonel McComskey Plaza and Berth's Garage, an ironic pairing that
> combines images of _____. The garage faces
> west, the way all America did in the days of _____
> _____. There we meet Flick Webb, the ex-basketball player
> who never did anything else. He works in a place that helps other
> people _____, but he goes nowhere. The name of the
> garage suggests _____, while
> Flick's own last name suggests _____.

However, I am always aware that Updike didn't write it for this purpose, and that the students will not make it their own for the purpose of the AP exam.

The ones who never leave are dismissed as losers by students convinced that they themselves will all move on to bigger and better things, but moving on is no matter to be taken lightly. I also ask students to think of friends and relatives who have gone on to college, jobs, or the military. When they come back to visit, they have changed.

They have changed for the same reason Odysseus and Huck Finn and, sadly, Mr. Kurtz have changed. They have been forced to make choices, and make them without the safety net of parents, teachers, religious mentors—coincidentally, all those people the students say they are anxious to escape. Only choices made away from that safety net can define a person, choices based on a realistic accounting of one's own values and with an acceptance of consequences.

Odysseus's name gave us the term for this life journey, a journey in literature that is physical and metaphoric.[2]

This is the Odysseus who devised a clever stratagem for ending the dispute between Helen's suitors, and when the stratagem backfired and led to war, he became literature's first draft dodger. This is the Odysseus who, upon arriving at Troy, made sure his ship was anchored dead center in the line. The Trojans would have to burn a whole lot of ships to get to his. This is the Odysseus who came up with the horse idea and who was so pleased with himself for all his human intellect that he felt no need to sacrifice to the gods before sailing home. He's in for a long trip, and he will be a different person when he's done.

To keep the length of the trip from bogging us down along with Odysseus, one of the bunch of bards who became "Homer" hit upon the brilliant idea of beginning in the middle of the thing, just as Odysseus's son Telemachus, grown to manhood in dad's absence, sets out to find his father.

What neither father nor son knows, but we do, is that Telemachus has been sentenced to death by the suitors. This adds a note of urgency to what Odysseus had begun to treat, thanks to Calypso, as a bit of a Mediterranean cruise. Even in the arms of a goddess, Odysseus still yearns to return to his home, his wife, and the larger world of real people—surely one of literature's earliest cautions about the limitations of empty sex. However, with his son in mortal danger, Odysseus will have to do more than yearn, and he will have to do it soon.

Still, the students wonder what Homer is trying to tell us with all the flashbacks to Polyphemus and Scylla and Charybdis and the

appreciation for Beyoncé. His roommate answered, "But she's black."

My student was dumbfounded. How could anyone not think Beyoncé was pretty? His roommate, equally perplexed, wondered aloud how any white person could think a black girl was pretty.

"I remembered what you said about *The Odyssey*," my student told me, "and at that moment I was looking at a Cyclops."

This roommate's opinion was unlike anything he had ever experienced. He was on his own. Only his internalized values told him to confront the other student, which he did, rather than just giggle along in hopes of acceptance.

When Odysseus meets Nausicaa, he has been through what would appear to be everything. He's been sunk again. He is naked before the princess, literally and metaphorically, with only "his ready wit and his knowledge of men." Ultimately, this is where we find ourselves at some key moment in life, when on our rite-of-passage journey we have to make a choice, and nothing we have been before—in Odysseus's case (and you can put them on the blackboard) leader, hero, smart guy, ace lover—matters at all. We have to look inside and see what resources we really have.

When Odysseus finally gets home he is a changed man. He cries. He takes on the identity of a commoner—a beggar. He is humiliated by the suitors and has to accept that humiliation. He is touched by the loyalty of friends and the love of family. Then he kills everybody.

Students have a hard time dealing with this. Odysseus had changed demonstrably. There is less that is clever and more that is emotional in the last third of the book. However, Odysseus's wrath at the suitors seems disproportionate. After all, some of them were mean to him when he was disguised, but not all of them. Don't people earn points for not being as bad as other people? Do they all deserve to die such horrible deaths?

Yes. All of them are guilty of the same thing. They all decided to stay home, to avoid the journey—any journey—with its new experiences and strange, dangerous choices. These young men are all from good families, and they seem very free of parental influences.

Yet their freedom has come at no cost and now requires that they do nothing but sit in someone else's house, living off his life.

Of course, even Updike's ex-basketball player, even the ones we identified so knowingly as losers, do not deserve to be shot. However, it is the nature of the suitors' crime that they have opted out of life. They have chosen not just to live off the larder of Odysseus, but to coast through existence without doing those things that make us truly alive. They've chosen a kind of death even before they are dead. The sad truth is that many people do this. There are a lot more suitors than there are heroes, and most of us will play the suitor game at some point in life.

The Odyssey is not about a single choice but rather about a life of choosing. The rite of passage may come to an end like a book, but the spirit of that rite of passage is what sustains. Without it, Homer might be saying you may as well be dead.

Tennyson's "Ulysses"[4] is a good companion piece, extending Odysseus's story into old age. He is now a king to a people who do not know him. He has "become a name," surely a familiar sentiment in our own culture of personality. But the voyage never ends, and he's ready to sail again, "For though we are not now that strength which in old days moved earth and heaven, that which we are, we are, one equal temper of heroic hearts, made weak by time and fate, but strong in will, to strive, to seek, to find, and not to yield."

The final line is more than a great example of the power of iambic pentameter. It is a testament to the continuing obligation to make the most of the hand we have been dealt, right to the very end. Yet another treatment, this an answer to Tennyson, is MacNeice's "Thalassa," which ends not with iambic confidence but with equal determination: "Our end is Life. Put out to sea."[5]

The odyssey of Huck Finn[6] is even more accessible to the typical student. His life is like all too many high schoolers' lives—torn between the contradictory value systems of two people who lay claim to his care. The widow represents civilization but also repression for Huck and slavery for blacks. Pap represents freedom and frontier survival skills, but also physical cruelty, and his skills will not take him beyond the sinking riverboat. (The Walter Scott reference is vintage Twain, but his antipathy to the Scottish author takes too long to explain to students.)

Torn between the two sets of values, Huck cannot take it, and he lights out, only to be thrown in with his spiritual father, Jim.

On his journey, Huck will meet monsters—surely nobody could argue that Colonel Grangerford is any less a horror than Polyphemus, all the more so for his humanity. Ultimately, Huck will have to make a choice about values, and that choice is clearer than anything in *The Odyssey*.

The chapter that nails the distinction between Twain and Huck on the issues of voice and of race is chapter 14, with its debate over the need for different languages among men. Huck cannot convince Jim that just as cows and pigs have different sounds, so too should men, and he concludes in disgust that blacks are unteachable.

As offensive as the language is, the message is clear. Huck doesn't get it. When I ask the class for Twain's point, I often get a well-meaning student who says that Huck doesn't understand that blacks have not had the same educational opportunities as whites. I nod appreciatively until another student raises his hand and gives the real answer, that Huck just doesn't understand that all men are created equal.

The issue of voice—of Huck's voice, and opinions that differ from Twain's—is settled. Is there a better illustration of how to make use of a first-person narrator? More important, however, we accept Twain's teenager's lack of awareness underneath the bravado.

The next chapter is a direct extension of this one. Huck needs an object lesson. He gets it when he is lost in the fog and returns to the raft—the center of his universe—only to find a bereft Jim, and teases him for his joy at being reunited with Huck. When he gives up the joke, Jim tells him he is trash for doing that to a friend.

It is worth noting that Huck, though a teenager, would be considered Jim's superior, and that Jim's comment, if overheard by other whites, would be reason enough for Jim's being lynched. I remind the students of Maya Angelou's poem about a cleaning woman, where she says, "the child I works for calls me girl."[7] Jim's lesson registers with Huck, however. As Huck says, still using the "n" word, it took him a long time to go and humble himself to Jim, but he does it.

It is good to see Huck get his comeuppance, but what can nonracist high school students get from this? The answer comes in their immediate experience. It doesn't take many questions for them to make the leap from the physical fog engulfing Huck to a more metaphorical one. He paddles around the island on a dark, foggy night, not sure where the current is taking him and increasingly aware of his own impotence. He has reached a point in his rite of passage where he feels lost, particularly when separated from the raft. For reasons he cannot quite explain, he is terrified.

Teenagers will show a great many emotions to avoid having to admit that they are terrified. They will put on an act toward friends, family, and teachers. This is what Huck is doing. It is easier at this point in his emotional growth to play a joke—particularly on a friend—than it is to admit an uncomfortable feeling. The response from Jim not only teaches him the limitations of his own racial view but also shows the limitations of this classic teenage coping strategy.

Huck is soon put to the test when a group of slave catchers approaches the raft. Huck shows his knowledge of people by begging the men to come aboard, and when they react with suspicion, he confesses that his "father" has smallpox. In one of Twain's wonderful ironies, the slavers respond as Huck expected (how sad to see a fourteen-year-old so knowing), but then turn his expectation on its head by sliding him a twenty-dollar gold piece.

This is the second of three very specific opportunities where Huck is given the option to turn in Jim. It is the first time he really thinks about the choice, but what he has learned of Jim's humanity in the past two chapters makes it impossible for him to choose slavery for the man he unconsciously but accurately identifies to the slavers as his "father."

It was around this time that Twain started having difficulties writing what was now clearly no longer a sequel to *The Adventures of Tom Sawyer*. He sinks the raft, and Huck, like Odysseus before him, is cast ashore with only his wit and knowledge of people to sustain him. He comes upon the Grangerford house, and his first inclination, as always when he is onshore, is to assume an identity—to hide who he is. The Grangerfords make this all too tempting a prospect.

Huck is paired with an alter ego, Buck, whose clothes are the same size; and Huck seems to have landed in heaven—a heaven still as much of a dream for far too many high schoolers—with a stable, cultured, yet strong family. It is everything he has ever wanted, and it is presented to him without the need for any choice on his part. He need simply continue to deny who he is, what his relationship with Jim has made him, and go along with the Grangerfords. He is, for a time, a willing suitor and is too immature to recognize the ominous glorification of death in the hilariously awful poetry and charcoals of Emmeline Grangerford.

Huck's first description of Colonel Grangerford is unwittingly laced with observations that should give rise to concern. Huck innocently notes that the family arrives for church and a sermon on brotherly love armed to the teeth. Of course it all ends badly, with Huck starting a massacre by passing a love note in a prayer book. He ends up back on the riverbank, looking at the body of Buck, of his alter ego, appropriately floating in the river, which has been Huck's vehicle for his rite of passage. Thank goodness Jim has arrived and rebuilt the raft.

Of course, a raft can only go downstream, decidedly the wrong direction for Jim. Twain will try to solve his logistical problem with an unsatisfying device of bringing Hannibal to Huck in the person of Tom Sawyer. Before that, however, students can find the book's true conclusion, when Huck tears up his letter.

It takes a bit of explanation to remind students of the reality of Huck's belief: a child of his times, he has been taught that stealing is bad, and on his journey has seen the damage thieves and charlatans can do. He believes he has stolen Jim from a person who never did him any wrong, and that the sin is compounded by his knowledge that Jim intends to free the rest of his family. He honestly feels he must return Jim to slavery in order to be redeemed. He goes so far as to write a letter telling of their whereabouts. He tears up his letter, however, and specifically declares his willingness to go to hell.

Here is the novel's real lesson for high schoolers. We do not achieve freedom just by declaring our independence. This can be an empty act of defiance. We do not become an adult just by moving away. Parents usually have just had to pay the dorm fee. We do not even achieve adulthood by rejecting the values we have had drummed into us. That's the easy part, and it is often accompanied with self-congratulation. Students become a full-blown member of the human race when they:

- encounter the new and different,
- remain open to the experience,
- recognize their choices,
- discard outworn dogma,
- substitute their own beliefs,
- act upon them,
- and—finally and most important—accept the consequences for better or worse.

Students can eventually acknowledge all these steps. It takes a few minutes of questioning, and it fills a blackboard, but it's worth it.

Not everyone can get there. Kurtz in Conrad's *Heart of Darkness*[8] illustrates a part of the rite of passage that we do not like to think about, that no eighteen-year-old wants to consider. What if one embarks upon that rite of passage, confronts the new, discards old dogmas, looks inside for the true "stuff" of his nature in order to plot his future course, and finds nothing there? We like books where the happy happens, or at least where the unhappy is heroic. This is not one of them.

If this book is taught in high school at all, it is most likely excerpted in conjunction with a social studies lesson in colonialism. There is nothing wrong with introducing a little of the hideous history of the Belgian Congo (the pictures in Adam Hochschild's *King Leopold's Ghost* are quite sufficient)[9] and with reminding students how colonial practices planted the seed for much of Africa's current tribal violence. However, reducing the book to a tract on the evil and hypocrisy of colonialism strips it of any universality, of any chance of rewarding students for this difficult read with anything relevant to their lives.

The group of men to whom Marlow tells the story, which will be retold to us, does not belong at sea. They represent positions of power in Victorian Britain, at a place and time that must have seemed as if it were the center of the world. Conrad had certainly seen it as such when he left his home at an age not far from that of our students to remake himself into a sea captain, a writer, and an Englishman. Little wonder that one of Conrad's favorite subjects was the person who reinvents himself.

As they sit in the Thames waiting for the tide, however, Marlow reminds his audience that this too was once a place of darkness. Hadrian's Wall was a remote and unsavory outpost of the Roman Empire, as dark as "darkest Africa," and, I remind my students, Westchester County, New York, was a land of wolves and Indian massacres much more recently.

Of course, more important than any comparisons between "darkest" Africa and any other place is the comparison between the real "heart of darkness" in the souls of people. As Marlow describes his own trip to the deathly headquarters of the company, to the coast where a ship full of European sailors is being killed by microbes, he responds with a pointless bombardment of the jungle—up the river through increasingly bizarre attempts to make European sense and order out of European repression of Africans. And he is not just exposing the evils of colonialism; he hasn't yet confronted the real point of the book.

He only starts when his steamer passes a village and he sees howling natives, describing them with typical European racist distaste. His horrific epiphany, however, is not that the people are like him, but that he would be no better than they, and probably worse, if he were free from the fetters of his own civilization. Kurtz's tragedy is that he arrives well meaning and intent upon being both a good company man and an enlightened master.

When he is freed from European restraint, however, unlike Huck with the benefit of Jim's instruction, he has no beliefs to take the place of the affectations, pieties, and cultural trappings of Europe. He has no "true stuff" inside.

Kurtz becomes more savage than any of the "savages" the Europeans observe. He is worse than any because he actually perverts their hero worship and leads one tribe to slaughter another. He does not do it for money or advancement, though the only reason "the company" has become concerned is that the ivory has stopped coming down river. He does it because he can.

Chinua Achebe, who dismisses Conrad as a racist, notes, "travelers with closed minds can tell us little except about themselves."[10] European lack of awareness of the achievements of sub-Saharan African civilizations certainly allowed for racist assumptions. Conrad's alter ego Marlow shows no appreciation for anything but the savagery he perceives. However, his real horror is in the savagery of the Europeans to which he bears witness.

In a rite-of-passage story, the only thing we have any interest in knowing about is what is going on in the mind of that traveler. The traveler, whether it is Odysseus or Huck Finn or Kurtz, is not traveling to learn about other cultures, but to learn about himself. That's the point.

Just as *Heart of Darkness* would have little resonance if it were only an exposé of imperialist exploitation, it would say little to today's readers if it were an accurate depiction of African culture circa 1899. David Denby's "Jungle Fever"[11] (reprinted in Moore's *Heart of Darkness, A Casebook*) provides an interesting account of a Columbia University seminar class's responses to *Heart of Darkness*. One student concludes, "the only common ground we have is that we can glimpse the horror."

Freedom from restraint is not enough. For some, it is no more than a license for barbarism, and the road to that hell is often paved with good intentions. Kurtz has just enough self-awareness left to appreciate the enormity of his crime, "the horror." The whites on Marlow's riverboat, who gleefully shoot the natives who have gathered onshore to witness Kurtz's departure, have no such awareness. They are disgusting and pathetic.

Kurtz is tragic. He is the Jedi master who has gone over to the dark side. These are some pretty fine moral distinctions to put before high schoolers, but the question of what keeps us from choosing badly, the nagging doubt of what lies inside us as well as in front of us, are real concerns for an eighteen-year-old.

I have every student choose from the following list the statement that best states the theme of Kurtz's story in *Heart of Darkness*.

They all vote and then we discuss the answers. (The best answer is number four.)

1. A man goes on a rite of passage and emerges a better person after acknowledging that the African natives he sees along the riverbank are just as human as he is, despite his European culture and sophistication.
2. A man goes on a rite of passage and is freed from the constraints of European civilization by the emotional freedom of the natives he meets on the riverbank. He can now feel again.
3. A man goes on a rite of passage and realizes he cannot accept the natives he meets on the riverbank as human. His obvious racism is his heart of darkness.
4. A man goes on a rite of passage and finds himself freed from all the restraints of civilization, but without any real belief in anything, he finds that his freedom is a curse. He can give to the natives on the riverbank, who at least know who they are, nothing but his own unshackled savagery.
5. A man goes on a rite of passage and learns to be a better person by realizing that he cannot "judge a book by its cover."
6. A sophisticated Englishman goes on a rite of passage and has a moment of inspiration on a riverbank when he realizes that the natives are no less civilized than his European ancestors were at one time.

With *Heart of Darkness*, I read Tim O'Brien's short story "The Sweetheart of the Song Tra Bong" in his collection *The Things They Carried*.[12] It is a grabber. There is also an excellent anthology titled *Leaving Home*, edited by Rochman and McCampbell,[13] with short rite-of-passage stories by famous authors, including O'Brien.

Mary Ann, only weeks out of high school, goes to Vietnam to join her high school sweetheart at a remote military base. "This seventeen year old doll in her god damned culottes, perky and fresh faced, like a cheerleader visiting the opposing team's locker room." Just as "all Europe contributed to the making of Kurtz," she is a product of every American cultural cliché. However, she gradually sheds her Midwestern ideal of a marriage, kids, and a picket fence, and succumbs to the attraction of the jungle.

She starts with what appears idle curiosity, but soon is going on patrol with the Special Forces and sporting a necklace of human tongues. She eventually disappears into the jungle. Her high school experience, her American culture, had left her, like Kurtz, with nothing real inside with which to confront new realities. It can happen.

The rite of passage is a theme that resonates with young people for precisely the same reason that it can appear as a motif in literature from Homer to Huck Finn to the present.

Teenagers go through traditional rites of passage in summer camp and in church or synagogue. These are traditional public acknowledgments of the child's passage to membership in the adult community. Unfortunately, many of them would now see violence, sex, and substance abuse as rites of passage. These are made to seem initiation rites into a group that only feigns adulthood for the benefit of peers and advertisers. They are cultural blandishments, horrific Kurtzian reminders that freedom from restraint is a long way from true independence, on a road fraught with peril.

These books are difficult but rewarding reads that can touch a real nerve with a modern teenager and can let him or her know that others have been there before. Ultimately, there is nothing high schoolers long to do more than achieve autonomy. They really do suspect that there is more to achieving autonomy than what they see on television. And there really is nothing they fear more.

Notes

1. John Updike, "Ex-Basketball Player," from *Collected Poems 1953–1993*. New York: Alfred A. Knopf, 1993.

2. Homer's *The Odyssey*, H. D. Rouse (trans.). New York: Signet Classics, 2007.

3. Jeanette Wintersoon, "Strange New World." (A review of Margaret Atwood's novel *The Year of the Flood*), *New York Times Book Review*, September 17, 2009.

4. Alfred, Lord Tennyson, "Ulysses." In Robert C. Pooley et al. (eds.), *England in Literature*. Glenview, Ill.: Scott, Foresman, 1963.

5. Louis MacNeice, "Thalassa," in *Louis MacNeice Poems Selected by Michael Longley*. London: Faber and Faber, 2005.

6. Mark Twain, *The Adventures of Huckleberry Finn*. New York: Bantam Classic, 2003.

7. Maya Angelou, "When I Think About Myself," in *Poems*. New York: Bantam, 1986.

8. Joseph Conrad, *Heart of Darkness and the Secret Sharer*. New York: Signet Classic, 1997.

9. Adam Hochschild, *King Leopold's Ghost*. Boston: Houghton Mifflin, 1999.

10. Chinua Achebe, "An Image of Africa, Racism in Conrad's 'Heart of Darkness.'" *Massachusetts Review* 17, no. 4, 1977.

11. David Denby, "Jungle Fever," in Gene M. Moore (ed.), *Joseph Conrad's Heart of Darkness, A Casebook*. New York: Oxford University Press, 2004.

12. Tim O'Brien, "The Sweetheart of the Song Tra Bong," in *The Things They Carried*. Boston: Houghton Mifflin, 1990.

13. Hazel Rochman and Darlene Z. McCampbell (eds.), *Leaving Home*. New York: HarperCollins, 1997.

Chapter Three

---○---

The Quest
Arthurian Legends, *Siddhartha,* and *Song of Solomon*

What am I looking for in life?
Is selflessness old fashioned?
Can our struggles make us noble?
Can our struggles cripple or empower us?

IN QUEST LITERATURE, the journey is still the vehicle for choice and growth, but now the journey is undertaken for a purpose. Something is sought, though it might be the wrong thing, sought in the wrong way.

In Mallory's version of the grail legend,[1] most of the knights of the round table are seeking something they know they cannot attain: only Galahad could sit in the seat perilous, and only he can completely experience the grail. In *Siddhartha,* the title character seeks enlightenment but cannot find it until he stops looking. In *Song of Solomon,* Milkman goes in search of a bag of gold and finds something worth much more. The three books could not be more different, and the notions of personal sacrifice, delayed gratification, and the value of a humbling experience could not be more irrelevant to the modern teenager—or so it would seem.

Writers who did not set out to be writers, from Chaucer to Conrad, have a place in my heart. In addition, depending on who tells the tale, Mallory wrote *Le Morte D'Arthur* while under an indefinite sentence for stealing horses, punching out a sheriff, or just being on the wrong side in a dynastic dispute. Mallory, even in modernized prose, is a tough read; however, the fantasy crowd eats it up, at least in excerpts. The basic premise is one we spend a lot of time debating: people should spend all their efforts striving for a perfection they cannot attain, and the more unattainable it is, the more selfless and noble the striving.

Arthur gets his knights around that round table by offering them something previously unheard of in the feudal system, which students have seen in social studies. He offers them a new way of doing business, based on idealism rather than power. They are not to serve a lord if he is venal, with the promise in return that they will be able to rule the serfs. They are to protect precisely those people who typically get raped and pillaged.

We talk about the Kennedy Camelot, and it takes a bit of a stretch now to conjure up the idealism of that age fifty years past, an idealism that brought "the best and the brightest" into government service and gave birth to both the Peace Corps and the Green Berets. It's even harder for students to think of our current public servants as idealists rather than ideologues, as selfless rather than self-interested.

We read a *USA Today* article titled "And It's All Legal"[2] that describes the ways in which congressmen can enrich themselves, putting relatives on lobbyist payrolls, taking "educational" junkets to London or Las Vegas. We compare these practices to Kennedy's inaugural address, with its call to "ask not what your country can do for you." I ask the students to imagine an American government of either party that really tries to serve the best interests of the people without any concern for staying in office. We talk cases, and the students smirk knowingly.

It is interesting, however, to watch their faces when I ask them to consider how they would feel if they could believe that a Kennedy Camelot were still possible. Some of them say they would still rather be millionaires, but many of them argue that they would like to feel idealistic, would like to devote themselves to service if they thought it was possible to do good. It remains to be seen if the Obama presidency will increase student optimism and involvement.

I suggest that Mallory might have felt the same way. Why his fascination for these ancient myths? By his time, had ideas of chivalry and nobility already become the butt of jokes by the cynical? After all, he was a knight himself, "Sir" Thomas, though the world he conjured in *Le Morte D'Arthur* was one in which a knight's calling was as different to him as it would seem to us. Locked in his prison cell, did he let himself imagine what a world of selfless idealism might be like?

Then there's the subject of women. The knights are supposed to devote themselves to a woman precisely because there is no chance that the woman will reciprocate with any affection. What a concept. The story of Beaumains, fighting one bloody battle after another for a woman who does nothing but insult him, should lead to a point where the girl will realize his worth and treat him accordingly. It never happens.

This is not the stuff of Hollywood or MTV. Again, we talk of why there is nothing particularly noble about sacrifice if it is undertaken to win some prize, whether that prize is a hot date or the National Honor Society. Is sacrifice really sacrifice at all if it is done for anything but a selfless purpose? Again we talk cases, and again, at least some of the students wonder what such a world would be like what they would be like in such a world.

Of course, it is up to them to make that world, and that itself is impossible. However, this need not lead to cynicism. When Arthur's knights seek the grail, the round table is already showing signs of trouble. Petty jealousies have arisen, Mordred is around to remind Arthur of Arthur's own moral weaknesses, and Lancelot and Guinevere are up to something—though what exactly depends on whose version of the legends one reads. The point may be that Arthur's knights, having striven for the idealistic in this troubling world, have gone as far as they can go, even in Camelot. Hence, the quest for the specific goal of the grail.

The Da Vinci Code has awakened new interest in what the grail might have been, but there is an even more interesting universal question at the bottom of all this. Why seek something you cannot find? Some of the knights literally kill themselves going after the cup that Galahad is destined to find. Two interesting ideas come out of this and lead to lots of discussion. The goal, the cup, the brass ring, the college admission, is not where one wins or loses. We prove ourselves on the journey—a journey we have already seen not everyone is willing to undertake.

The harder we try, the better we are, and, once again, the more difficult—even impossible—the goal, the more noble our effort.

When Galahad finally "wins" the cup, a strange thing happens. His spirit floats away, accompanied by a band of angels. The message here is a bit of a comfort for those of us who are not Galahad the Pure. When you are as pure as he was, you are not really human. Galahad cannot stay with Bors and Percival because he is no longer one of them—one of us. He has entered a state to which we can aspire but which, as long as we are to remain fallible human beings, we can never attain. The surviving knights are better for the effort of the quest—and they get to remain people for a while longer.

The quest for "the impossible dream" is apparent in Cervantes's *Don Quixote*—another tale about knights written in a time when knighthood had lost much of its meaning—and in *Man of La Mancha's* most famous lyric. This is also the message of *Sir Gawain and the Green Knight*.

Playing around with the symbolism of *Sir Gawain and the Green Knight* is fun, and the careless readers will assume that the color green must symbolize envy because they have not gotten beyond the cliché. Even better readers, however, those who can reason to the correct association of green with the life force, will have a hard time understanding the sash across the shield—the green on the pentacle.

Isn't Gawain ashamed of himself? Isn't it a reminder that people need to watch out for their own cowardice and be less proud? It takes some questioning to get to the real point.

Arthur gets it, and the Green Knight gets it: the sash is a sign of honor.

I ask the students to consider what Gawain did. If an eight-foot-tall green monster interrupted my dinner with a challenge, I would gladly step aside. If I chopped his head off and he picked it up off the floor, I would be out of the hall in a shot. If I was supposed to go meet him at his place to get my own head chopped off, I would spend a few weeks riding around in the woods and come back to Camelot saying how sorry I was that I couldn't find the fellow. If I found the courage to go look for him, and the beautiful lady of the castle offered me wealth and companionship, well . . .

Gawain does all the right things and a lot more than most of us would have done. The one thing he will not turn down is the green sash that will keep the life force going, that, quite literally, will save his neck.

The color green symbolizes life in all its verdant richness, and life is what no real human being will lightly dispense with. Gawain declines the opportunity to "do a Galahad." He wants to stick around, just shy of perfection. I cannot blame him, and neither can Arthur. As both Shakespeare's Lear and Heller's Snowden teach us, "ripeness is all."

The enduring lesson of this and the rest of the Arthurian legends is that we should strive for perfection, but given an honest effort, we should not kill ourselves for coming up short. We will do better next time. The wonderful echoes at the end of Mallory are not for the once and future king who will return to save England, but for the possibility of a world where we all try to be as good as we can. Why else would Hollywood, the Broadway stage, children's books, and video games still evoke the memory of the round table?

A deceptively easy read is Hesse's *Siddhartha*.[3] I inherited a closet full of dog-eared copies when I inherited the class from a retiring teacher, and I had my doubts about the book. It seemed a relic of the 1960s, and I wondered what students of a different era would make of a quest for the meaning of life set in ancient India. I sold the students short in this, and the book remains one of their favorites.

Writing in the wake of World War I, Hesse could have written a book about a young man wandering Europe in an attempt to fill an empty soul. Hemingway did this in *The Sun also Rises*; Maugham did this in *The Razor's Edge*. However, like Mallory, Hesse sought out a long-lost, largely apocryphal past. His Siddhartha makes for good reading in November of senior year, as students are trying to present themselves as candidates for college admission and are looking over their achievements with a critical eye.

Siddhartha is an admissions counselor's dream: he's brilliant, handsome, healthy, hard working, and his parents are Brahmins with enough money to endow a department. When it comes to fate, did anyone ever have more luck in the gene pool sweepstakes?

And he chucks it all to become a samana. I tell them to imagine they are going home that night to tell their parents they have decided to skip the whole college thing and become Hare Krishnas.

Siddhartha, however, then becomes the perfect ascetic, out-samana-ing the samanas. It is assumed he will take over the group, but, having learned what he can from this phase of his life, he leaves. For an encore, he meets Buddha and rejects him as a teacher, and then he meets the courtesan Kamala and proves to be a sex machine, and then he meets the businessman Kamaswami, and becomes the equivalent of an arbitrage genius or dot-com whiz kid. He can't lose, and yet he's never happy.

Some interesting questions are posed by the simple language. Siddhartha questions whether Buddha's teaching that all things are connected and ongoing can be true if the goal of Buddhism is to separate from precisely this. This is perceived to be a flaw in Buddha's teaching, but what of the Christian belief in God as "proven" by the Uncaused Causer? If God must exist because all things must be caused by something, who caused God? Faith is a matter of believing what cannot be proven. That being said, is any faith worth killing someone?

Philosophical fine points notwithstanding, the real reason for Siddhartha's rejection of Buddha rings true with students: no teacher can teach the way to enlightenment. One of my students pointed out Buddha's saying: I can point you to the stars, but do not confuse my finger with the universe. To listen with an open heart is one thing, but no student should surrender a shred of his or her uniqueness to any teacher, even the Enlightened One.

The most interesting thing about the character is that he keeps looking for meaning, not because he is unsuccessful, but because his success leaves him unsatisfied. My students are at a juncture in life where rejection and failure have become more real to them than ever before, even in the competitive feeding frenzy that is the typical adolescent's world before the college search begins. If this guy can have all he has and still seek this thing called meaning, his quest deserves to be taken seriously.

Siddhartha's problem is a peculiarly twentieth-century one, a peculiarly Western one, a peculiarly familiar one to the high school senior. He compartmentalizes everything. He devotes just enough effort to one thing to be able to squeeze out all that he perceives as useful, and then it's on to the next thing. The sum of the parts never adds up to anything.

Look at the typical high school student's day. Classes are divided into increments punctuated by bells: time to leave French for chemistry, chemistry for social studies, to sit in each classroom in the same seat, even if never officially assigned, with the same view of the classroom. Then there's the time to be spent on the track team, the school play, the part-time job. Then there's the homework, again a piece of this and a piece of that, along with the college essays, the campus visits, the whole packaging bit. Then there's time to slot in for friends and family.

Then there's the bigger picture, where school years add up to a completed high school experience, to be followed by four years of college, to be followed by—what?

Their younger siblings are programmed into playdates and lessons and practices and games and recitals. A look at their parents shows much of the same. Parents have their friends from work, and their friends from the neighborhood, and their friends from among the other parents. They have specific time allotments for every waking moment.

When does the high school student even sleep, let alone dream? *Siddhartha* is all about the need to put things together, to see connections—something the high school experience has been designed to preclude. As we discuss the book, the students realize that they were not even aware of what a gigantic source of frustration their own overprogramming has become. They become positively wistful as they imagine having the time to think about their activities not as a résumé list but as a life, to see themselves as acting in a process, a pattern of growth, rather than reacting to a fear of failure.

Siddhartha finally gets off the merry-go-round he has created for himself. He experiences a midlife crisis, when he realizes he has lost the youthful zest for truth, knowledge, experience—life. I ask students if they feel about the world the way their parents do. The answer is predictable. I then ask them if they think their parents felt as they did when they were eighteen.

They are shocked by the notion, but they grudgingly admit that it may be true. Perhaps their parents are the way they are now precisely because they experienced what Siddhartha experienced—the realization that they were not the world-beaters they thought themselves at eighteen. How will our eighteen-year-olds deal with that realization if it is as inevitable as it seems? Must it lead to the death of dreams?

Siddhartha goes back to the river, a river that had previously been merely a thing to cross on the way to his next conquest. The ferryman, Vassudeva, who had told him he would return, now becomes a new kind of mentor. Now he stays put, and the whole world comes to him. Kamala comes through on her own quest but is bitten by a snake and dies. She presents him with his son, who rejects Siddhartha just as confidently as Siddhartha had rejected his own father. His friend Govinda, whom he had treated as an inferior intellect and had left with the unnecessary teacher Buddha, returns to help keep him from killing himself. Finally, he finds his truth in the river itself.

Sorting out that final chapter takes some real work. We talk about Siddhartha's comment that a rock (or a desk, or a piece of paper) must be respected not for what people can make of it but for what it is. We talk about the "om," the word that includes so many sounds—as long as it is not said perfunctorily, on the way to other words and events. We talk about how the river—real and metaphoric—is the same but always different. We are so much better at naming than we are at understanding, even at seeing. The river may be the same, but the water has fled downstream since we just stepped in. The contours are subtly different. A new fish has made an appearance.

Siddhartha had tried to separate himself from the world, only to then try to immerse himself in the world. Finally he has stopped looking for the meaning of life and finds it in a connectedness in all things, which transcends the things themselves.

We talk about how, to paraphrase Wittgenstein, the world is a collection of facts, not things. We compare the last chapter to the final lines of *Four Quartets*, from, "We shall not cease from exploration."[4] Both in theme and imagery these lines offer useful connections to Hesse.

Even without knowing the specific symbolism of the *Four Quartets*, the students always do an inspiring job of analysis, showing how far they have come from simple paraphrase: arriving back to a place and seeing it for the first time, finding a simplicity that costs everything, things not known only because they were unlooked for, the speech of children, the renewal of water, the reconciling of the seemingly irreconcilable.

We finish with a selection of quotations from Tolstoy to Nietzsche, my list simply culled from *Bartlett's Familiar Quotations*:

"Mankind a future life must have, to balance life's unequal lot."
    —Burton
"If you do not think upon the future, you can not have one."
    —Galsworthy
"The only significance in life consists in helping to establish the
    kingdom of God." —Tolstoy.
"I slept and dreamed that life was beauty / I woke and found that
    life was duty." —Hooper
"Life without industry is guilt; industry without art is brutality"
    —Ruskin
"Life's race well run / Life's work well done / Life's victory won /
    Now cometh rest." —Parker
"Is not life a hundred times too short for us to bore ourselves?"
    —Nietzsche

Each student picks a quotation and explains why Siddhartha would or would not agree with it. They are relieved to learn that there is no right answer.

The last quest we consider is Toni Morrison's *Song of Solomon*.[5] There is nothing deceptively easy about this read, but students often cite it as their favorite book of the year. Milkman goes in search of a bag of gold from a cave, the stuff of *Tom Sawyer* adventure tales. He finds instead that the bag contains bones and later finds that the bones are not those of a murdered white man but of his own murdered grandfather. He quests for gold and finds his heritage, that thing we all lug around with us as if it were a heavy sack, but which we often fail to recognize.

The book brings together many elements we have already studied. Like Homer's characters, Morrison's have a fascination with names. Names can be given, but they also must be earned. If Milkman is to shed the unfortunate associations of his nickname, he must earn the name of Macon Dead, a name that had itself been cobbled together by a drunken Union corporal, but which Milkman's grandfather had made a source of pride.

The power of storytelling is as much an issue here as it was in Conrad. Milkman hears stories from his parents, but they are contradictory and self-serving, venting the parents' hatred of each other and leaving Milkman feeling soiled and confused. In contrast, Pilate's stories and those Milkman hears on his journeys (notably from a character called Circe, an impossibly ancient crone who presides over a pack of dogs) fill him with a sense of pride and purpose.

Morrison imbues Milkman's growing appreciation for his past with all the joy and excitement of the uncovered mystery. These issues are rich in suggestion for high school students. Are they carrying around a bag of bones, the weight of ancestry?

What's in that bag, and not just as a burden but as something sacred and ennobling? From whence did they get their own names? What did their parents intend by those names? What of their nicknames? What did they do to earn them, and if they could, what new name would they give themselves as they go off to college and start with a relatively clean slate? What stories do they have in their family treasury? Who told the stories and why? What can the bad ones have cost them personally, and what can the good ones give them in return?

Song of Solomon works on many levels, pulling together the tragic and the comic, the allusive and the symbolic, the real and the magical, and nowhere is this more true than in the many references to flight, from the hood ornament on Macon's car to Pilate's name in its little box taking flight with the help of a bird.

Look at the scene where Macon takes the family to view some lakefront property. It works as a finely tuned delineation of family dynamic ("Not you!"), an accurate statement of racial awareness ("They'll like it if they own it."), a comic turn of situation and rhetoric ("I told you negroes don't like water."), and a profound presentation of theme ("as if there was no future to be had.").

Look at the development of a perfect simile: "The disappointment he felt in his daughters sifted down on them like ash, dulling their buttery complexions and choking the lilt out of what should have been girlish voices." A class period can be spent discussing how Morrison's precision wrings every bit of meaning from the image—and how true the image is in its depicting the brutality of parental disapproval.

One of my students recently remarked on the amount of anger in this book, and we discussed anger's corrosive power. From the Seven Days, to Circe, to the personal relations of Macon and Pilate, Macon and Ruth, Guitar and Milkman, anger generates much of the plot. Milkman needs his quest to break the cycle of anger, the poison that produced what he is—a self-centered and destructive character through much of the book. And what of love?

The last word on this is Pilate's, as her name flies to the heavens. Pilate has seen racism take her father, her beloved nephew take her equally beloved granddaughter, his friend take her life. Having given so much throughout the novel, her response is, "I should have loved them all."

Many of my students are already familiar with Hamilton's children's book *The People Could Fly*,[6] the folktale of the slaves who were gifted with the ability to fly to free themselves from bondage and fly to a home that had become for them a place of myth and longing. Milkman's great grandfather had that gift.

The poor Mr. Smith, whose "flight" opens the novel, bringing to an end his career as a life insurance salesman and a killer for the

Seven Days, connecting forever the lives of Milkman and Guitar, does not have the gift, though he obviously yearns for it. If Morrison's storytelling has convinced us of the reality of a woman with no navel, perhaps the power of the story is enough for us to believe that Milkman does indeed fly at the end, like his ancestors Solomon and Jake, enfolding his murderous brother in his arms.

Not that many years ago, Peter Pan asked our jaded teenagers to save Tinker Bell by clapping if they believed in fairies. A lot of them did. Despite how jaded they seem, they resent a world that has taken from them their capacity to wonder, to believe. They appear to sit stupefied in front of cable television, watching the expletive-bleeped, contrived passions that purport to comprise *The Real World*. How many of them would happily trade that reality for Harry Potter?

You can't go home again, but perhaps there is another choice after all. Perhaps after a few weeks in Camelot and ancient India, they are ready to save Milkman, and themselves, with the healing magic of the quest.

NOTES

1. Albert R. Kitzhaber and Stoddard Malarkey (eds.), *Arthurian Legends*. New York: Holt Rinehart and Winston, 1974.

2. Jonathan Turley, "And It's All Legal . . . ," *USA Today*, December 27, 2004.

3. Herman Hesse, *Siddhartha*. New York: Bantam, 1971.

4. T. S. Eliot, *Four Quartets*. London: Faber and Faber, 1970.

5. Toni Morrison, *Song of Solomon*. New York: Vintage International, 2004.

6. Virginia Hamilton, *The People Could Fly: American Black Folk Tales*. New York: Alfred A. Knopf, 1985.

Chapter Four

---○---

I Want a Hero
The Canterbury Tales, Beowulf, and Hamlet

What is a hero?
Why do we need heroes?
Do I want to be one?

A HERO IS what our cultural values tell us we should strive to be. In accepting the exemplar, we accept the values. Considering Beowulf, or Hamlet, or the firemen at the World Trade Center, or Mother Teresa, we can reconsider our own sense of what constitutes real courage and selflessness above and beyond the call. In literature, that sense can be found in a heroic response to events, leading to Homer's "some great deed that will be sung by men hereafter."

The first lesson is that very few of us are consistently heroic or antiheroic. Most of us are Homer's "suitors" most of the time. The general prologue to *The Canterbury Tales*[1] is instructive of the way society divides, five hundred years ago or five hundred years from now. Some people are very good, rather more are very bad, usually because they add hypocrisy to their list of sins. In the middle is a vast array of average folk who do the daily business of getting by and whose jobs sometimes lead them to compromise—to corner cutting—even if it is against their better nature.

While we can marvel at Chaucer's skillful depiction of several levels of fourteenth-century society, it is more instructive that he presents such a universal moral divide. As a storyteller, presenting

37

some of the characters he would have known all too well from the vantage point of his home above one of the gates into the walled city of London, Chaucer shows rather than tells.

Is the nun really a good singer who speaks French; what are we to make of her love of animals; and what do those rosaries tells us about "Madame Eglantine's" vows of poverty, chastity, and obedience? A closer look shows us that she sings through her nose, that her French is limited to the schoolbook, that she feeds her dogs better than the tithing peasant can feed his children, and that her coral beads end not in a crucifix but in a golden brooch inscribed "Love Conquers All."

Chaucer also matches the characters to the stories they tell. Consider how the Miller's Tale is precisely the kind of bawdy story he would have used to beguile the poor peasant while he leaned on the grain scales with a thumb worth its weight in gold. Consider how the Pardoner's moral tale of the three men who sought death is the perfect sales pitch for the fake relics hawked by this most unholy of men.

Consider the Wife of Bath's Tale with the answer to the question, "What does every woman want?" and with the correct response of the knight—a former rapist—when given the chance to dictate the kind of woman his wife will be. Raised on "The Frog Prince" and "Beauty and the Beast," every student anticipates that the knight will answer the old woman by taking her ugly and being rewarded with a beautiful woman, kind and faithful. The knight, however, has learned his lesson and lets the woman choose.

This message is still timely, but consider also how the whole story fits as an advertisement for the Wife of Bath—perhaps on the pilgrimage looking for husband number six?

Students can have fun making up their own list of pilgrims, using their own list of occupations—as well as their own speculation on what, if anything, would deserve a pilgrimage today. In addition to providing an appreciation for Chaucer's gift for showing rather than telling (oftentimes showing the opposite of what he seems to be telling), this activity makes students think about the what and why of the adult world, a world they are on the brink of entering.

Insist that one of their pilgrims is a member of the profession they think they want to join—not just the straw men of drug dealers and dot-com millionaires. Make them think of how ready they are for the world of moral ambiguity that awaits their heroic response.

Beowulf is a great heroic story, not only in the hero's triumphs but also in his acceptance of fate.[2] This is the story of the stranger who is like us but not one of us—the Geat come to save Denmark is not far removed from Shane or Superman, from a Jedi or a Jesus. The hero is brave not only in his self-sacrifice but also in his willingness to stand alone. His very heroism separates him from those he saves and the moment they embrace him.

I can still recite the opening voice-over of the television series *Superman*, "who came to earth with powers far beyond those of mortal men, and who, disguised as a mild mannered reporter for a great metropolitan newspaper, fights a never ending battle for truth, justice and the American way." As we huddled under our desks in 1950s schoolrooms, waiting for the Soviet missiles, we had reason to think our American way needed superprotection.

Today's students are well versed in the power of the comic-book hero and in the history of the genre. Indeed, when we first start talking about heroes, the first examples students give are from comics and graphic novels. If Superman was a creation of the 1930s, a time of Great Depression and the seemingly irresistible rise of fascism, what has given rise to the resurgence of comic superheroes today? Is there a similar feeling of hopelessness in the face of insurmountable problems? Was this a feeling known all too well to the "Dark Ages" author of *Beowulf?*

The Danes need Beowulf because their great mead hall, emblematic of their advancing civilization, was under threat, a threat none of the natives seemed able to handle. Grendel, a product of the swamps and a descendant of Cain, is forcing the Danes to abandon their Heorot and retreat back into the darkness.

In his three separate battles, the hero fights Grendel as a young, cocky stud anxious for fame; fights Grendel's understandably upset mother with an additional sense of obligation for the trouble he has caused, for the men he brought to Denmark, and for the fact that this time he might not come back; and fights the dragon to free his own people from the consequences of a slave's sin. If that last part sounds familiar, it sounded sufficiently familiar to the Christian monks who decided Beowulf was worth transcribing and editing.

The societal appreciation for the hero story as an embodiment of cultural values is certainly evident here. It is also evident in a fifty-line passage that interrupts the final battle. Wiglaf goes to Beowulf's aid, but before he does, he upbraids his comrades (who, like Christ's apostles, had bailed on him in the moment of truth, though the Bible shows most made heroic comebacks) and treats us to a long story of where he got his sword.

In this passage, which interrupts the narrative at a key point, we see many of the values of the old pagan culture, coexisting with the monks': the values of physical courage, responsibility, family honor, and the need to pass on something to the next generation. How far removed from the 9/11 firemen are these men of the "Dark Ages"?

Again, few of us are heroes. "The Wanderer" is an Anglo-Saxon poem about a follower. His leader has died, and the followers have been forced to disperse and wander the land in search of a new group. He passes mysterious ruins that he ascribes to giants but that we know were built by the Romans, at a time when this too was a place of darkness. A wise man reminds us that all things are only lent to us—friends and relatives included—a tough realization that students have to grapple with in times of death and divorce.

The saddest thing about the wandering is that different groups take the man in, but only for a night. He tries his best to be agreeable in hopes they will let him stay, and the one thing he can never do is let on about his broken heart, his insecurity, his fear of rejection. To reveal these emotions would be the kiss of death to any relationship, as any high school student knows who has ever tried to break in at a new school or with a new clique. These poets of the Dark Ages may have been ignorant of their own island's history, but they knew a thing or two about the fragility of relationships and the danger of showing who they really are.

When it comes to relationships, to the dangers of emotions, to the importance of the hero, who can beat Shakespeare? However, could even the Bard's fertile imagination have pictured the cottage industry of consultants advising on how to make him relevant to the modern student? At one such consulting session, a teacher volunteered that she began her study of Shakespeare with a lecture on E. W. M. Tillyard's *The Elizabethan World Picture*. At the other extreme, a consultant presented a series of three classes, full of groups and sharing, in which the students spent three class periods deciding what it was they did *not* know about Shakespeare.

Between these extremes there are a wealth of good things to do with Shakespeare, one dramatist who never lost the concept that we go to "see" a play, not hear it. Ultimately, however, the man had something to say, and we have to get around to it eventually.

In a recent *New York Times* essay on the Accelerated Reader system, now used in 75,000 schools, Susan Straight sadly pointed out that *Hamlet* was "worth" only seven points on Accelerated Reader's "readability rating," one point less than the Gossip Girl novel *I Like It Like That*.[3] The consultants notwithstanding, I have found that when it comes to plays that speak to the modern teenager, nothing, including *Romeo and Juliet*, beats *Hamlet*.

Hamlet[4] is about a bunch of college-age students (Hamlet, Horatio, Laertes, Rosencrantz, and Guildenstern are all students at Paris University or the University of Wittenberg, though admittedly older than today's undergraduates) who are making their peace with an adult world full of corruption and compromise.

While the gravedigger scene establishes Hamlet's age as thirty, it also provides in a single line much of the issue this very young man faces—an issue that makes him so approachable to today's college students. Watching the gravedigger pitch bones about, Hamlet and Horatio comment:

> *Hamlet:* "Has this fellow no feeling of his business? He sings in grave making."
>
> *Horatio:* "Custom hath made it in him a property of easiness."
>
> *Hamlet:* "'Tis e'en so. The hand of little employment hath the daintier sense."

Experience is a cruel teacher of the young. It, and only it, inures them to pain, to loss, to compromise. Hamlet is forced to get his own dainty hands dirty in order to fulfill his promise to his father. If only Claudius had let him go back to college in Act 1, Scene 2. Now, in Act 5, after the death of Polonius, the hoisting of Hamlet's school friends with their own petard, it is too late for him. Custom will give the nasty way of the world a property of easiness, even in the sweet prince.

I do not often share my life story with my classes, but I do mention that after college and graduate school, I came to understand *Hamlet* only after spending a few years practicing law. I had had a particularly horrible day dealing with abuse and neglect cases in family court. Back in my office, I started throwing files in disgust and found myself repeating the "What a piece of work is man" speech, which had been made into a song for the musical *Hair* (another story of college-age kids facing that adult world of corruption and compromise). My secretary looked at me as if I were crazy, which, in the best Shakespearean sense, I absolutely was.

The kids laugh, but the point is that *Hamlet* becomes real when that adult world smacks us in the face, and it smacks today's students in the face much earlier and graphically than it ever did to the rest of us. They need *Hamlet*.

Long before he finds out the truth about Dad and Mom and Stepdad, Hamlet feels a loathing for the adult world that comes out in his first exchange with his mother. He describes the outward show of grief that he eschews and ascribes by implication to his mother. "Nay, I know not seems," he says, with a sad, wise sneer that Holden Caulfield would know only too well. The adult world is full of phonies, his beloved mother included, and there is nothing that makes a young person angrier. Hamlet does not want what "seems." He wants the real deal.

Hamlet wants to know that people are being up front with him. As is the case with so many of our young people then and now, life is a pretty constant disappointment on this score.

Hamlet is as gifted a young man as Siddhartha—look how Ophelia describes him even after the nunnery scene. He is also an idealist with a sense of duty. He is ripe for heroism—and for tragedy. The adult characters are all phonies. This is obvious in the case of Claudius and, sadly, Gertrude, yet humorous in the case of Osric. It is most delicious, however, in the case of Polonius.

As Shakespeare so often does, he gives a villain a Hallmark card moment: "This above all, to thine own self be true." This bit, taken out of context, is the stuff of valedictory speeches. In context, however, it is all about watching your back, not being open with anyone, keeping up appearances. "Gee, dad, I'm off to college, to take on the world." "Sure, son, but don't get too excited and be too open with anyone or you'll just get screwed." It is good advice in the way of the world, but what kid, off to college full of hope and promise, wants to hear this? None of the students in front of me want to.

Unfortunately, Laertes has already absorbed much of the attitudes of his dad. His advice to his sister is even more accurate and more unwelcome and presumptuous. Any student can paraphrase the "open your chaste treasures to his unmastered importunity" bit, and no girl would want to hear it from her big brother. Again, it is predicated upon expecting the worst. Polonius makes this brutally clear when he adds his two cents' worth after Laertes departs. What girl would want her father to dismiss her first love, in effect saying, you think he loves you—what are you, a moron?

Later in the play, Polonius will go so far as to hire a spy to check up on his son and to instruct the spy on how to lie cleverly about Laertes' reputation in order to get at the truth himself. I ask my students to imagine their own parents doing this to them. What is rotten in the state of Denmark? Do not worry about what you do not know about the Elizabethan world picture. Take a look at the family.

Hamlet's own family situation is instantly recognizable to the contemporary teenager. He loathes his stepfather. Even before he hears from the ghost, he cannot understand how his mother, who loved his father, could so quickly marry his inferior uncle.

Even if it made sense politically—it did for Henry VIII, at least until he met Anne Boleyn—there is a disturbing lack of decorum in the haste. When he learns from the ghost that Gertrude had been conducting an affair behind her husband's back, it is almost too much. Hamlet had already compared the royal brothers to Hyperion and a satyr. To realize now that his mom had been with goat man even while she hung upon his father is a revelation that obviously affects him even more than the news of his father's murder.

How many young people, regardless of what they say, look upon the relationship of their parents as a model for what they will find in marriage? Hamlet thought he had a model for marital devotion; he finds a garden grown rank. The ghost never says Gertrude was even aware of, let alone complicit in, the murder plot, and the ghost warns the son, whom he knows all too well, to "Taint not thy mind with thoughts about thy mother. Leave her to heaven." However, when Hamlet insists that he will erase from his mind all books, all childhood memories, all hopes and dreams, and leave a blank slate for his father's command, the first thing he puts on that blank slate is "Oh, most pernicious woman."

The impact of the revelation is immediate. Hamlet begins by making his best friend swear a holy oath, implying that he can now trust nobody. He also states that he may have to put on "an antic disposition." The young idealist, who insisted "Nay, I know not seems," is prepared before Act 1 is over to put on a false front, to play the phony as well as Claudius can, to pretend to be that which he is not.

Hamlet must take on the real world in all its evil. As the prince and the murdered king's son, he has no choice but to act. The world is "out of joint" and he was born to set it right. To do so, he must fight it on its own terms; he must get his hands dirty with the mud of compromise and distrust. And what of our students? They, too, will have to find their way through the ethical quagmires and emotional disappointments. How much of their own idealism will survive when they must fight their own battles on the world's terms? A parent can only hope.

Of course, parents are at a premium in Hamlet. Hamlet's father is dead. Ditto King Fortinbras. There's no mention of Horatio's mom and dad, and no sign of Polonius's wife. Polonius will hide himself once too often behind a curtain—hiding what he really is so that Hamlet takes him for his better and deals him his fate. When we see how quickly Laertes and Ophelia fall apart after the death of their own father, we can appreciate the painful balancing act Hamlet has undergone since the death of his. The orphaned Fortinbras also waits in the wings.

The reactions of the young people put them in rather neat categories instantly recognizable to today's students. Faced with the realities of life, some young people will try to keep emotions at arm's length, treating problems like textbook questions—as Horatio does for a time. Some will do whatever they are told, just looking for the right angle—as Rosencrantz and Guildenstern do. Some will react with petulance, unable to address ethical concerns in a blind need to strike out at the unfairness of it all—as Laertes does. Some will simply disintegrate, withdrawing, sometimes permanently, from a world that punishes them for their sensitivity—as Ophelia does. Some will react with authority, imposing their own order on the chaos the adults have handed them—as Fortinbras does.

In being all of these things, Hamlet is none of them. As prince and son, he knows he must act. As a moral man, his one fear is that he will act unjustly. He tries to hold his emotions in check, though he finds it increasingly difficult, particularly when his own friends do him dirty.

"Were you sent for?" he asks the two school friends he will soon learn to trust as he would adders fanged. "I have of late, but wherefore I know not, lost all my mirth," comes from this exchange. (If you are in search of a modern, parallel text, look at the situation and imagery in Baraka's poem, "Preface to a Twenty-Volume Suicide Note.")[5]

"Where is your father?" he asks his girlfriend, and her blatant lie will set him off as little else has, leading to the violent part of the nunnery speech.[6]

Hamlet cannot help but be drawn down into the muck in order to fight his uncle. At the end of Act 1, he is already distrusting his friends, making them swear that holy oath rather than taking their word. He also admits that he will start putting on an antic disposition—pretending to be something he is not—this from the young man who knew not "seems."

Ultimately, Hamlet will do what Oedipus and Beowulf did. He will be defeated, but he will take with him the evil that has befallen his society. What makes this hero resonate with today's teenagers is no fight against a dragon, but a fight against himself. He is as proud of his fluency with language as any advanced placement student. However, he will come to have contempt for the kind of linguistic facility that masks the truth or that stands a poor substitute for actions.

There are times when life just plain stinks. Hamlet is no Galahad. He is one of his generation, heroic as he tries so hard to keep everything together and keep it real.

NOTES

1. Geoffrey Chaucer, *The Canterbury Tales*. New York: Bantam Classics, 2006.

2. *Beowulf*, Burton Raffel (trans.). New York: Signet Classics, 1999.

3. Susan Straight, "Reading by the Numbers." *New York Times*, August 30, 2009.

4. William Shakespeare, *Hamlet*. New York: Washington Square Press, 1992.

5. Amiri Baraka, "Preface to a Twenty-Volume Suicide Note." Retrieved from http://www.english.illinois.edu/Maps/poets/a_f/baraka/online poems.htm.

6. For examples of staging for this scene and equally memorable scenes from *Macbeth* and *Othello*, see John Russell Brown, *Shakescenes*. New York: Applause Theatre Book Publishers, 1992.

Chapter Five

––––––––––––◯––––––––––––

The Anti-Hero
Native Son and The Stranger

Can we learn from bad guys as well as from good?
Who does society fear and why?

THE HERO EMBODIES the best we like to think we can be. The anti-hero likewise makes us reconsider our values, again because of the character's response to events. While youth culture at first seems to provide many candidates for anti-heroism, students know that the in-your-face singer or actor of this week will be the overpackaged millionaire of next week. In literature, the answer is seldom as easy as it looks.

Two characters who are opposites that arrive at the same place are Bigger Thomas from Native Son[1] and Meursault from The Stranger.[2] Both men are anti-heroes: random killing is not yet a behavior lionized by our culture. However, their stories make us consider values, just as surely as the stories of heroes. Society hates what it fears most. It chooses to crush Bigger, for an accident rather than a murder; it chooses to crush Meursault, not for shooting a man, but for failing to exhibit proper emotions. In asking why, we find out a great deal about ourselves.

We are not supposed to want to emulate what Bigger Thomas or Meursault do, but we do have to ask what exactly they have done to bring down upon them the wrath of their cultures. Society reveres the hero's actions as embodying our best human reaction to crisis. However, it reviles the anti-hero not because it loathes his actions but because it fears his attitudes.

The first scene of *Native Son* never fails to grab. An alarm goes off—a wakeup call to everyone—and four people in a tiny apartment are attacked by a huge, yellow fanged rat. Bigger kills the rat, but the foreshadowing is all too obvious: he, too, will do what comes naturally to him, will attempt to escape, will fight back, and will die, having earned no more sympathy and having evoked as much visceral terror and revulsion as did the rat.

The first section of the book rings true in so many details: the symbolism of the double feature Bigger sees—blacks in the jungle and whites in the cocktail party; the psychological reality of Bigger's avoiding the robbery by picking a pointless fight; the irony of his wanting to be an airman and becoming a chauffeur; the hypocrisy of Mr. Dalton, who makes a fortune from the rat-infested apartments and then donates a ping-pong table, who sends blacks to school but will only hire them as servants; the metaphoric as well as physical blindness of Mrs. Dalton, who can't see where her family's money comes from.

My students really loathe Mary Dalton. Poor, doomed Mary? Yes, indeed. High school students know what a phony she is, and worse than that, what danger she represents for Bigger. On his first night on the job, she makes him disobey his orders, tries to get him drunk, makes him take her and her boyfriend to a soul food restaurant, and makes him take her home so plastered that she has to be carried to her bedroom. She does all this to show how down she is with her black brother, without the slightest recognition of his acute discomfort, and without the slightest regard for the increasingly compromising positions in which she places him.

She does not deserve the death penalty for all this. The point, however, is that neither does Bigger.

Bigger smothers Mary by accident when her blind old mother wanders into the bedroom. From that point on, he is a dead man. We cannot help but root for Bigger to get away, but one of the truly heroic things Wright does is take away our sympathy for him, so that we must root for him for Wright's reasons, and not out of any patronizing, Mary Dalton–ish sense of righteousness. Chopping up

Mary's body is a gruesome scene, but it pales in significance to the murder of Bessie. Fearing capture, Bigger hits his faithful girlfriend in the face with a brick, then throws her down an elevator shaft to die a slow death.

Wright forces us to accept Bigger for what he is. He won't let us—as Bigger himself will not let Max—treat him as a victim of society. To do so would reduce him to something less than a man, or at least to the level of Lennie in *Of Mice and Men*—a victim of cruel circumstance and his own limitations. To be full-fledged human beings we must have the power to act and the power to choose. We must have the power to accept the consequences of our choices. That brings us back to Huck Finn.

This is not to say that Bigger is not a victim of society; it is just that he refuses to be limited to this role. That his trial is not about justice is abundantly clear when he is convicted of rape, with no possible evidence, and convicted of a murder that was not a murder by any legal definition. Even more to the point is the way Bessie's murder is treated. She is wheeled in as a piece of evidence, an exhibit, only to show how Bigger could have been depraved enough to kill Mary.

Bigger's deliberate, vicious murder of his lover is not a crime to his society, yet that society demands his death. Why? What is it that he represents that is so horrible as to be intolerable? Society cannot allow him to be a man.

In court, the prosecution insists he could not have been smart enough to fool the police on his own with the fake ransom note. But he was. Meanwhile, his own lawyer insists he should not be held responsible for his actions because of society's greater sin toward him. But Bigger insists he should. Just as Wright eventually rejected communism, Bigger ultimately rejects Max's help. Before the novel, which began with a "ring," ends with a "clang," Bigger's simple assertion that he did not know he was alive until he felt something strong enough to kill for reduces the prolix Max to stumbling, despairing silence.

Camus's Meursault will also insist on standing alone, on facing the reality of the action rather than the unreality of fake emotion. However, Camus's anti-hero is in a very different position from

Wright's. Meursault is a Frenchman, a colonialist, who kills an Arab, a native, a person of not much more concern to his colonial society than Bessie was to her society. Why then must he die? What Meursault's society finds so repulsive is not the action but the lack of emotions that surrounds it.

He must die because he refuses to feel what we desperately want him to feel. Those feelings are necessary, not just to make the act of killing bearable, but more so the act of living.

While I hasten to assure my students that I am not trying to dissuade them from their religious beliefs, I ask them to imagine the consequences of a world without God. Two consequences are pretty quickly apparent. First, why should anyone be good if there is no entity to demand obedience to moral law? Second, what is the point of our existence if it is not to get us ready for another existence?

These are tough questions, and only humans are lucky enough to be beset with them. The squirrel outside the classroom window is not paralyzed in his nut gathering or squirrel making with thoughts that this will all someday be over for him. He does not worry about making the world a better place, being kind to other life-forms, or establishing the significance of his own existence.

People choose to eat of the fruit of the tree of knowledge, and what we know is that we are going to die. In fact, after the forty minutes of a class period is over, we are all forty minutes closer to the moment when we will run out of minutes. We cannot have the minutes back, so it would be nice to feel that we have something to show for them.

What if we treated every class period that way? What if we treated our whole lives that way, demanding significance or at least being more aware of the facts of our existence?

As most people haven't the stamina for all that, we have resorted to a number of devices to insulate us from the truth, to keep us in squirrel land, if you will. Some might say—I try not to say it myself—that this is the function of religion, of Marx's opiate of the masses.

What about popular culture? One need not look to dystopian fictions like *1984* or *Fahrenheit 451* to see that our culture keeps us rather pleasantly unaware by keeping us awash in the right kind of feelings. Wear the right shoes or drive the right car and you can have a false sense of belonging; watch the shouting matches of "reality television" and you can have a safe, vicarious outlet for anger; watch a snippet of news or a made for television movie about famine relief or conjoined twins and you can reassure yourself with a cost-free sense of sympathy and righteousness.

Most important, express the right feelings yourself and look for the same expressions in others, and we can all tolerate this life of ours. "I'm so sorry for your trouble," "You look great," "I'm feeling fine," "Everything will be all right." The typical high school student's day is as full of these lines as any adult's.

Meursault will have none of this. When Meursault's boss offers him a step up the bureaucratic ladder with a promotion to Paris, Meursault would rather have the sun and the beach. When his girl-friend asks him if he loves her, he says he doesn't know what love means, but if she wants to think so that's okay.

Then we have the famous first lines of the book and the ciga-rettes smoked at his mother's vigil. It really doesn't matter to Mom when she died now that she's dead. To whom does it matter? It matters to all the rest of us who are depending on the superficial exchange of sympathy, of expressions like those of the director of the funeral home. "Deepest sympathy." Who are we kidding? How-ever, we omit these expressions at our peril. As Camus says in his notebooks, Meursault is "a saint of negation."

This extends even to his own defense. The class is set the task of defending Meursault, without changing any facts. Here's what we end up with for a closing argument:

> Poor Meursault, already distraught at the death of his mother, is confronted on the beach by an angry Arab. His friend pulls a gun, but Meursault, the peacekeeper, takes it from him so no one will be hurt. Later, feeling unwell, he goes for a walk on the beach. He doesn't even realize he still has the gun. He is confronted again by the Arab. He is not a man of violence but he is alone and frightened. He pulls out the gun only when the Arab threatens him with deadly force—a knife gleaming in the blinding sunlight. The gun discharges, and, shocked with nervous energy and terror, Meursault continues to jerk the trigger. Later, utterly distraught at what has happened, he is completely cooperative with the police.

These are the facts. What we have added are emotions, emotions Meursault did not feel, but we dearly wish he had. Consider the stories in the day's newspaper. The murder that chills is the one that is without apparent motive. The killer who chills is the one who is without apparent remorse. Even murder can be made palatable if it's surrounded by the acceptable emotions that keep us from confronting unfortunate things—like death, the Arab's or our own.

Consider the murder in Czechoslovakia, described in a news clipping Meursault finds under his prison bed. Is it worse than the crime Meursault committed? If so, why? Is it because of the relationship between killer and victim? Is it because it was done with a hammer rather than a gun? Is it not worse because there was a motive? Even Meursault thinks the victim deserved his fate. But where in all this is the fact of killing, the ending of life? What really matters here?

We are back to the nurse's comments at the funeral—walk too slowly and risk sunstroke; walk too quickly and risk catching a chill in the chapel. We all end up in the same place. Life is about facts—we exist, and then we don't.

Is knowing our lives are finite not an awfully depressing thing? Remember Woody Allen's joke in *Annie Hall* about the two women at the hotel: one complains about the miserable food, and the other agrees, adding, "and such small portions."

We are given what seems an awful lot of minutes at birth, and we spend them recklessly and often with little return. If we were given a million dollars and told that we would never have another cent in life, how would we spend it? Would we be less careless if we knew we could never get more? So, too with life. We spend our minutes as carelessly as we do an allowance at the mall, only because facing its finiteness is too scary a proposition.

If this seems too depressingly negative a way to frame the case, consider an alternative. What if we remembered "The Wanderer" and its admonition that friends are lent, kin are lent? What if we embraced the proposition that this finite life was all we had and demanded that our life be lived, as the existentialists say, authentically? What, on a day-to-day, class-period-to-class-period, hour-to-hour basis, would an authentic life be like?

Two modern poems on the subject of finality and its effects are Wallace Stevens's wonderfully poignant "Waving Adieu, Adieu, Adieu,"[3] and section XVI of Mark Strand's *Dark Harbor*.[4] By all means read the poems for examples of technique such as internal rhyme, but also consider the crucial question of whether the awareness of endings leads to crippling sadness or to a more profound appreciation for the importance of all things.

This still leaves us with the question of morality. Meursault, saint of negation or not, is not a hero. Why shouldn't we find our authenticity in sitting on our balcony smoking cigarettes (Meursault would probably have died of lung cancer in a few years anyhow) or in shooting people? Camus had an interesting answer. In his notebooks, he said, "We should serve justice because our condition is unjust, increase happiness and joy because the world is unhappy. Similarly, we should sentence no one to death, since we have been sentenced to death ourselves."[5]

We should be just to one another, precisely because there is no divine justice? Because we are all in this together, and we are all we've got? Think about that one.

Who is the really just person, the one who is just because he fears injustice or because he seeks a heavenly reward, or the one who chooses justice with no concern beyond justice itself—that is, authentically? Isn't this the same spirit that motivated Arthur's knights, that belief in the good action becomes more noble the more impossible it is to seek reward? Bigger and Meursault are no knights of the round table. They may not seem to stand for much, but they stand in defiance against societies that find it comfortable to stand for nothing.

Asking students to name their heroes is asking them to state what they stand for. Many will point to the firemen at the World Trade Center or to Mother Teresa, to people who embody values we would like to think we could exhibit on our best day. Sadly, many students jump right to the comic superheroes. They are not necessarily expressing cynicism about today's people as much as they are expressing fear over the pervasiveness of today's problems.

Often the hero has come from afar with ability beyond our own, like us but not really one of us, like Beowulf, like Shane, like Superman, like Jesus.

Consider again Clark Kent. There's a guy who could take care of Osama bin Laden and probably fix global warming and racism by dinnertime. Our popular culture is going through a phase right now where comic-book heroes are once again in vogue. Look at what is playing at the multiplex and ask if students are not ready to tackle some real ideas about what makes a hero and why we need them—now more than ever.

NOTES

1. Richard Wright, *Native Son*. New York: Perennial Classics, 1998.

2. Albert Camus, *The Stranger*. New York: Vintage International, 1989.

3. Wallace Stevens, "Waving Adieu, Adieu, Adieu," in *The Collected Poems of Wallace Stevens*. New York: Vintage, 1990.

4. Mark Strand, *Dark Harbor*, XVI. New York: Alfred A. Knopf, 1993.

5. Albert Camus, *Selected Essays and Notebooks*. London: Penguin, 1970.

Chapter Six

———————◯———————

Literary Devices

Why not skip the books and talk about the ideas?
Why does careful reading matter?
Doesn't analysis spoil the fun of reading?

REALLY GOOD LITERATURE is not just about the themes of the works. If it were, there would be no real point in reading the books at all. You could discuss the ideas without ever having read a page. (Some students will try. I once received an essay where a student desperately tried to remember what we had talked about relating to *The Canterbury Tales*, while struggling to mention two characters—General Prologue and Bath's Wife.)

Of course, students read the things we give them because they have to. They do not walk into any class looking for life changes. They walk in looking for fun with their friends, amusement, and a passing grade from me. Therefore, unless they can be inspired to feel that reading matters, they will read as little as possible, as quickly as possible, with as many shortcuts—yes, Cliffs Notes, SparkNotes—as will allow them to get on to as much of calculus and French that likewise stand between them and graduation. How, then, can they be convinced of the need to consider not only literary themes but also literary devices?

We compound the problem if we only use literature, particularly poetry, as "discussion starters," reading only as deeply as we need to in order to elicit a personal response. We can encourage students to read more closely if we can empower them with a simple appreciation for technique, with a confidence in their own ability to analyze without esoteric technical vocabulary, and with an understanding that good writers use literary elements to make their point. Otherwise, what is the point?

Without an appreciation of how the parts fit to make the whole, students' analysis tends to focus on one point and spin a hopeful interpretation from there, ignoring the linguistic evidence in the rest of the work. Early in the year, I draw a huge circle on the board and a tiny box within it. I put my face up to the board at that box and say, "I'm not going to look at this big nasty circle, but I see this! I can write like heck about this!" The result of such analysis is an essay such as one student wrote with the help of his father. The father admitted that he thought "Dover Beach" must be about the famous White Cliffs, so he figured the ignorant armies part must have referred to the Battle of Britain.

I then fill that big circle with words like meter, structure, diction, and symbol and try to present the students with some useful means of real textual analysis, without ever calling it such.

As a student myself, I used to find it difficult to believe that authors existed, that *Ethan Frome* and *Julius Caesar* are the fruits of real human imagination, and not just the mandatory verbal pushups trundled out each year from the musk of the book room. However, in order to make the real human concerns of the author more profound, it sometimes helps to understand that even the way they wrote was a matter of conscious choice. "They do it on purpose" is one of my themes. However, even if they do it on purpose, if they don't do it for the purpose of enhancing their ideas, it's just showing off.

For example, what is the point of talking about meter? Do we have to memorize the names of all the metrical feet? Who cares about iambic pentameter? Nobody cares, unless its use somehow makes it easier for me to understand or feel something that affects me.

I give students the line from Gray's "Elegy Written in a Country Church Yard": "The plowman homeward plods his weary way."[1] Someone always manages to figure out what a plowman might have been and what plod means. I then tell them to rewrite the line, using only Gray's exact words. After I get a few suggested reorderings on the board, we stand up and start to move around.

First we plod in iambic pentameter. Then we stagger drunkenly to "Homeward his weary way the plowman plods." Then we march to the tune of "The Campbells Are Coming" to "His weary way homeward the plowman plods." The words are telling us that the plowman is plodding, but the meter has him practically skipping home. This will not work. Wow, we must have iambic pentameter!

Read the last lines of Wordsworth's "Michael"[2] and Tennyson's "Ulysses"[3] and see the very different effects of iambic pentameter.

What about verse forms? Of course, form can be something as simple as why "Dover Beach"[4] begins with a real beach before going to a real beach with a fictional scene, before going to a beach on the Sea of Faith. Hold the page at arm's length. The poem is in four parts— why? Why not three? Could the order of the parts be reversed?

The poem presents three beaches. One is a real beach that the speaker and his love are looking at as he speaks. The second one is the Aegean, a real enough beach, but the setting now is a hypothetical visit from the playwright Sophocles. The third one is "The Sea of Faith." Try finding that one on a map. What if we began with that one, with a philosophical metaphor? How would that affect the emotional and intellectual impact of the poem?

Clearly, we receive help from the earlier description of Dover Beach, with the pebbles being dragged back and then thrown up only to be dragged back again. That vivid image lets us know what Sophocles is so sad about, that eternal note of sadness that comes from the inexorable two steps forward and two steps back of human "progress." This early sharing of insight between real people on a real beach helps us care that the Sea of Faith is evaporating, as we move gradually from the concrete to the abstract. The poem then returns to Dover and the poet's plea that the lovers be true to each other, because there's not much else.

This raises some interesting issues among teenagers. What did we learn in *Othello* about being disappointed in life and throwing everything into a relationship? The value of the question, its importance in human experience, justifies at least a moment's awareness of how clever Arnold was to structure the poem the way he did.

Form can also be as simple as why Keats's "To Autumn"[5] is in three parts, indicating three aspects of the season and three times of day, each with its own type of imagery. To the student who asks if all this is really just subjective and how can we know what any of these people were thinking, "To Autumn" offers the perfect corrective, as Keats was kind enough to write a friend about the poem he had just finished. The real answer to that perennial student question is that the evidence is in the techniques.

I use Strand and Boland's *The Making of a Poem*[6] to make students consider form. I give them Roethke's poem "The Waking," tell them it's a villanelle, and then ask them to come up with the rules for this verse form. Once we have the basic rules (nineteen lines, five stanzas of three, a final of four, first line of the first stanza is repeated as the last line of the second and fourth, etc.), we reread the poem and ask the important question.

What does the verse form contribute to the meaning of the poem? The same with Bishop's "One Art," and Thomas's "Do Not Go Gentle." What does the repetition of key lines in this very restrictive form do to enrich the subtle differences in the lines' emotional impact?

I give them Kees's "After the Trial," and do the same exercise for a sestina. As always, the ultimate question is what the poem is about and how the form helps to convey this.

The one form students think they do understand is the sonnet. Everyone knows they are fourteen lines long, and advanced placement students know they are in—yes—iambic pentameter. But why? Why write a sonnet?

Shakespeare, of course, wrote lots of them. "When in Disgrace with Fortune and Men's Eyes" rings true in theme with many high school students. We spoke earlier about the idea, but why is this idea perfect for expression in a sonnet?

The first four lines describe a familiar situation—the kid who feels worthless, who flunked the test, got rejected from college, missed the free throw, and got dumped by his girlfriend a week before the prom. The second four lines show the worst thing a person can do in such a situation, but the most likely thing that people do, in fact, do—the kid who wishes he were somebody else, this guy over here who aced the test, this guy who never misses a free throw, and so forth. But then something happens in line nine.

It begins with "But." It only takes one person who thinks you're not so bad, and then you can accept yourself again. In fact, if that person means enough to you, you wouldn't think of being anyone else, because anyone else wouldn't have that person's acceptance. This is why people write sonnets: to pose a question, complicate it, and then offer a "but." Could anything appeal more to an emerging adolescent mind?

One of the first poems we read is Frost's "Design." Unlike Shakespeare, Frost did not write a lot of sonnets, so, if he did this on purpose, that "why" is particularly significant. The first four lines describe a spider carrying a dead moth. The next four lines inch us in a direction we do not want to go, with imagery that confuses our sense of what is pure and innocent and what it dark and sinister. Line nine hits us with the real question. Why was that flower an abnormal color, what made that spider camouflage himself there, and what steered the moth in his direction?

"What but design of darkness to appall," says the poet, adding with a chilling dismissiveness, "If design govern in a thing so small." It's not much of a leap of vocabulary to connect design with fate. Of course, if design governs the moth, what else does it govern?

Here we have a white-haired man on a farm in Vermont debating issues of fate versus free will, divine versus human responsibility, as if he were Bigger Thomas or a character in *The Odyssey*. But why the sonnet? Eventually we get to it. A sonnet cannot be what it is without satisfying a lot of rules.

It cannot be fifteen or thirteen lines long. It has to have iambic pentameter, rhyme scheme, octave, and sestet. It has more design to it than any other kind of poem in English. The form underscores the theme of the poem. It requires that we give ourselves up to the pattern, just as the arrangement of Frost's little triumvirate does: flower, spider, moth. If design govern a thing so small. We do not just see the idea; we see how the form makes the idea so much more powerful.

Questions of diction and tone are hard for students to grasp in a literary context, but certainly not in a social one. I remind them of every parent's favorite complaint: "It's not what you said that was so bad—it was the way you said it." If the way you said it was so important in your refusal to clean up your room or eat your dinner, why shouldn't it be worth considering in the writing of Shakespeare, or Austen, or Toni Morrison? Diction is simply choice of words, but it takes students some time to realize that listing a bunch of words and saying what they "mean" is not diction.

Diction, like symbolism, deals with gut issues. A great poem for illustrating this is Seamus Heaney's "Blackberry Picking."[7] Read the poem and ask one simple question: what are words like "blood," "fur," "rat grey," "lust," and "clot" doing in a poem about children's blackberry picking? Maybe the poem is about something else? Look at the language and you see it is not a poem about how berries rot. It is a poem about how even innocent youth will grab for too much and in their lust for picking will bring about the inevitable souring of the long-anticipated experience.

Similarly, look at Hardy's "The Darkling Thrush."[8] The language choices in the first two verses are all about death. Why "spectre grey" rather than some other shade of gray? The word choices of the second two verses are full of references to religion. Why evensong and carolings? Still, the final image of the poem is ambiguous. Does the thrush's attempt at song fill the speaker with joy or just serve to confirm his pessimism?

Of course there is room for individual interpretation, but students should be made to support their assertions. I encourage them to believe that there is always an answer, but that it is seldom the first, most obvious thing.

Diction gives us tone. What do parents mean when they warn "Watch your tone of voice"? Your decision to emphasize certain words in certain ways can change something sincere into something sarcastic. Ask Holden Caulfield. In addition, the author might be setting up a narrator to make his own point. When Huck says of the "Ode to Stephen Dowling Bots, Dec'd," "If Emmeline Grangerford could make poetry like that before she was fourteen, there ain't no telling what she could a done by-and-by," he is being completely ingenuous. Twain means for us to hear something else.

Diction and tone really matter to *Hamlet*, because they really matter in any tale of cruelty or corruption. They matter in every high school hallway and in every household. They matter in every place of business—but students will learn that soon enough.

Students are even less aware of the fact that prose writers use literary devices. The prose writer must be just as adept as the poet at using structure and symbolism. To illustrate the former, I present an "instant story" in a list of events as follows:

1. boy wakes up, eats Cheerios
2. goes to school, can't find girlfriend
3. on his way to first period, friend says girlfriend is dumping him
4. sits through first period, can't concentrate
5. goes to English class, sees girlfriend sitting inside
6. she sees him in doorway, turns away
7. English teacher demands homework before he can enter
8. boy stammers a plea that he be allowed in before the bell
9. English teacher insists he hand in homework before admission to room
10. student hits teacher with copy of *Ethan Frome*
11. student subdued by classmates
12. taken away by police in squad car

We start with all the different possible points of view: the boy, the girlfriend, the teacher, the friend who told him about the girl, the teacher of the first period class, Mom or Dad, the policeman, student who helped subdue him, an innocent bystander in class, Edith Wharton. What would be gained by telling the story from each perspective and what would be lost? How would the theme change depending on whose story it is: the bad choice (the boy), consequences of a careless word (friend who told), I didn't see it coming (teacher), the danger of obsessive love (girlfriend), kids these days (policeman), and so forth. At what point should we enter the story (Cheerios, police car, moment of the assault, moment the boy is told)? It's all about choices.

Then there is the symbolism. How could symbolism enhance the story? I stole a lesson from a workshop years ago, and if I could remember the name of the presenter I would gladly credit her. She showed us a series of greeting cards, congratulating people on the birth of a child. I now have my own collection.

The boy cards usually show a young boy, not an infant, engaged in shooting a sling shot, throwing a ball, exploring a stream, and so forth. The girl cards show a baby and emphasized pretty faces, tiny feet, and passivity. "Whatever he touches, whenever he speaks, wherever he goes, whatever he seeks," said one (blue, of course) boy card, making the infant sound like Tennyson's Ulysses with his "to strive, to seek, to find and not to yield." One girl card was nothing but an infant dress, in pink, with a label "It's a girl." No, it's a dress. But the point is not that card makers do this on purpose but that writers do, so how does this translate into storytelling?

Since our instant story is set in a classroom, we have to decide how we want the reader to feel about that room. We could tell the reader what to feel, but the symbolic is more effective. I ask the students to look around the room and find physical things that could suggest that the classroom was a stultifyingly dull place where no idea had caught fire in years.

The list is embarrassingly long: the tired paint, the locked cabinets where knowledge is kept under the teacher's key, the windows with their broken shades that offer a drooping frame for the real world, the posters that are the same as last year's, the ceiling tile that hangs precariously over a student's head, the fluorescent light that makes all things beige, the floor tiles in their symmetrical arrangement. If this were how the setting was described, how would the reader feel about the class, about the teacher, about the students' predicament?

Then I reverse the process. Take the same room and now find details that suggest something worthwhile is going on. This is tougher sledding: the board full of notes, the window that opens onto the world, the locked cabinets where precious books are safeguarded, the teacher's desk awash in student work.

The point is to get students away from the multiple-choice definition: a symbol is something that stands for something else. A symbol is something concrete that helps us to feel or understand something abstract. Authors use them on purpose.

Look at Tim O'Brien's very short, short story "The Man at the Well."[9] Almost every physical item in the story—guns, uniforms, hoop earrings, well water, flies, blind eyes—carries symbolic weight, and when a soldier bloodies a peasant with a milk carton, there is a stomach-turning awareness of irony and corruption, not only for a generation raised during the Vietnam War, but from a generation raised on "Got Milk?" billboards. Of course, it was Lady Macbeth who spoke of "the milk of human kindness."

The inevitable question is whether looking for technique ruins the ability to "relate to" a story. We remember Emily Dickinson's "If I read a book and it makes my whole body so cold no fire can ever warm me, I know that is poetry. If I feel physically as if the top of my head were taken off, I know this is poetry. These are the only ways I know it. Is there any other way?" I assure them that if they once get the trick of seeing things on different levels, they will see more, not feel less.

All too often students are invited to do little more than share their similar experiences or "respond" to what they think is the theme of a work. Surely there is nothing wrong with responding to literature—that's the point of this book. However, we do students a disservice if we do not also make them more discriminating, sophisticated readers. We do this by teaching literary devices.

When we approach a story from the question "Why did he do that?" and then assume, "She did it on purpose," the author's choice—from Homer's structuring his poem from the middle of the thing to Brontë's use of a narrator—is not a daunting issue for any high school or college student, as long as it is clear that there is an idea, a real human issue, behind each choice, and not mere artifice—the author's or the teacher's.[10]

Asking merely "what" the author said will always lead to paraphrase, and paraphrase is not worth much on an AP exam or in life. Asking "why" an author said something and "why" he or she said it that way will lead to analysis. In a recent class, we had discussed the obvious symbol of the scarlet letter as it related to plot and theme. Just before the bell, one student summarized things better than I had: "I get it," she said. "Plot is about them; theme is about us."

NOTES

1. Thomas Gray, "Elegy Written in a Country Churchyard." *The Oxford Book of English Verse*. Oxford: Oxford University Press, 1955.

2. William Wordsworth, "Michael." Retrieved from http://www.bartleby.com/41/372.html.

3. Alfred, Lord Tennyson, "Ulysses," in Robert C. Pooley et al. (eds.), *England in Literature*. Chicago: Scott, Foresman, 1963.

4. Matthew Arnold, "Dover Beach," in Robert C. Pooley et al. (eds.), *England in Literature*. Chicago: Scott, Foresman, 1963.

5. John Keats, "To Autumn," in *The Oxford Book of English Verse*. Oxford: Oxford University Press, 1955.

6. Michael Strand and Eavan Boland, *The Making of a Poem*. New York: Norton, 2000.

7. Seamus Heaney, "Blackberry Picking," in *Selected Poems 1966–1987*. New York: Farrar, Straus & Giroux, 1990.

8. Thomas Hardy, "The Darkling Thrush," in *The Oxford Book of English Verse*. Oxford: Oxford University Press, 1955.

9. Tim O'Brien, "The Man at the Well," in *If I Die in a Combat Zone*. New York: Laurel, 1987.

10. A very accessible book on poetic technique is Paul Fussell's *Poetic Meter and Poetic Form*. New York: McGraw-Hill, 1979.

Chapter Seven

———————○———————

A Woman's Place
Medea and *A Doll's House*

Why do women ask, "Are you strong enough to be my man"?
Does hell have no fury like a woman scorned?
Where can a woman find justice in a man's world?
What if she makes her own justice?

TWO OF THE MOST famous plays about women rebelling against male-dominated societies were written by men, Euripides and Ibsen.

Thumbnail sketches of the history of drama tell us that Euripides differs from Sophocles in that he is more interested in the depths of the human psyche than in the airing of moral questions. His people speak about their relationships to one another, more than about their relationship to the gods and their plans. No psyche can be more terrifying than that of Medea.[1]

The Greeks knew the story of Jason, the ultimate Greek hero, and aristocratic Greeks tried to trace their family trees back to his Argonauts. But lurking in the shadows of the heroic tale was the knowledge that Jason would not have gotten that golden fleece without Medea, and that he and his Argonauts would not have made it home without her willingness to chop her little brother into pieces and throw the bits overboard for her angry father to stop and reclaim. Medea is a non-Greek, a "barbarian" in the truest form, and anyone who has ever been new to anyplace can appreciate her alienation.

Anyone who has been introduced into a new social group at school by virtue of a new relationship can appreciate her dependence on Jason. When he dumps her for a real Greek princess, and has the gall to tell her she should thank him for making her a pseudo-Greek, when he berates her for her passionate extremes and says she should be more moderate, we share her anger and her loathing of the thing she once loved.

This is no woman to trifle with, however, and her revenge is as disproportionate as was her love. When she kills her rival, and her rival's father, we can understand her actions, even if her motives would not pass muster in a court of law.

We are back to Bigger and Meursault. As long as we can ascribe motive, causality, to her vicious acts, we can fit them into a context, be saddened but not shocked by them, repulsed but not terrified. We can impose justice with understanding, and we can even congratulate ourselves for our own right decisions and for the moral order of the universe we inhabit.

Then she murders her children. This is beyond us, beyond our ability to rationalize. This threatens us in primal ways we do not want to face.

Sadly, we see current examples in the news of fathers killing their families. The stories are reported one day and forgotten within a few days. Every few years, a woman kills her children, and she is on the cover of a newsmagazine, which gives birth to pundits leading us in a round of national soul-searching. Why the difference?

One theory advanced during the Susan Smith murder case was that women have the gift of life. It is the number of women who can bear children, not the number of men ready to sire them, that determines the growth of the race. There is no need to be clinical about it; the math is fairly obvious. If women have this power over the future of what we still call "mankind," what would happen if they discovered the power to destroy that life?

It is no accident that the sorceress Medea strikes a bargain for sanctuary with the king of Athens by offering her aid in his efforts to produce an heir. She has powers that Greek men do not possess, a propensity to passionate excess that Greek men cannot tolerate, and now the ability to take from Greek men their children—even those she herself bore. This was a scary prospect for Euripides' audience—then as now.

There are more modern analogues. Some accounts of the seventeenth-century witch hysteria in Europe and the Americas note that much of the violence was directed at traditional folk healers—mostly women—who threatened the authority of doctors and clerics—all men. Today, while many men and women are opposed in varying degrees to abortion, the ones who feel compelled to attack people because of the issue always seem to be men.

While we may be tempted to apply to Medea the old bromide "Hell hath no fury like a woman scorned," we might also consider that hell itself offers our culture no more horrors than those presented by a furious woman bent on controlling death as well as life.

On yet another level, Medea looks forward to Othello and his loving not wisely but too well. It is the unequivocal nature of her passion that makes Medea powerful in love and hate. She comes from Colchis, on the eastern shores of the Black Sea (a look at a map will remind us that this is a part of the world that still resists Western efforts to understand, let alone tame, it). For all Medea's scheming, she offers nothing but truth and will accept nothing less in return.

Greek society—arguably all society—depends on subjugating pure, unrestrained emotion to the moderating forces we call civilization. Where do we draw our lines? What prevents us from resorting to barbarism (literally, non-Greekism)?

In addition, hasn't youth culture always championed honest emotion as the antidote for hypocrisy, duplicity, timidity? Remember Hamlet and his "nay, I know not seems." How can emotional honesty, even taken to extremes, ever be wrong?

We take a look at e. e. cummings's poem "since feeling is first."[2] Surely this is the accepted poetic view of emotion. The blood approves of dismissing syntax and seeing poetry itself as not worth an "eyelid's flutter," when that flutter says we absolutely exist for one another. What teenager, what adult, would not consider kisses a better fate than wisdom? But are there really no limits to the supremacy of emotion? This is Euripides' question in *Medea*, Shakespeare's in *Othello*, Brontë's in *Wuthering Heights*.

Cummings has his answer, and the poem is a delight. Certainly we want to believe in the poem's final dismissal of syntax, that given the power of love, death itself is "no parenthesis." However, if the answer were easy, humankind would not have wrestled with it through the ages.

I can remember feeling that way when I was young, though, thankfully, I avoided Medea- and Othello-like excess. I find that I now put more stock in wisdom, even in syntax. It is interesting that so many teenagers do so as well, their song lyrics notwithstanding. Perhaps we have forced them to become more pragmatic and literal at a young age. As much as they dream of love, they fear a world without restraint, a world where Medeas can, and do, happen.

Ibsen's *A Doll's House*[3] is a more acceptable account of justified indignation at male dominance. Like Jason, Torvald is arrogant in his feeble superiority and soul deadening in his reverence for conformity. Nora's response is not to kill her children, just to leave them, in order to find herself. In fact, Nora's response is so acceptable to the modern audience that some discussion of how unacceptable it was in nineteenth-century Scandinavia is necessary for the play to have any bite.

The play is available in several film versions, including one with Jane Fonda and David Warner and the other with Claire Bloom and Anthony Hopkins. The latter is closer to the play, though both have their merits. As with most plays, I like to have the students act out improvisations of the situations, followed by actual scenes, followed by class discussion, followed by viewing the same scene played differently by different professionals.

I also like to walk through the experience of seeing a play (again, we see a play—we don't go to hear it). In a real theater we would browse through our playbills. A casual look at the cast of characters would tell us that this play, like *The Glass Menagerie* or *Fences*, is a play about family, as opposed to one about community like *The Crucible*. As we usually see the set before we meet the characters, it too raises certain expectations. With one student reading the set design notes, and with the rest of the class directing me, I draw a rough sketch of the set on the board.

Then we discuss our feelings about what it reveals about the Helmers. We usually conclude that the room is "just nice," and never was that expression more appropriate and more damning.

Into this world comes Nora, playing games with her children and deceiving—innocently for the moment—her husband. It is hard for students to act out with a straight face those scenes where Nora plays up to her husband, but it is interesting to see once the words are off the page just how much play is involved.

When the catalytic conflict—Krogstaad's letter—is introduced, some students have a hard time realizing that it is a big deal. In the larger scheme of things, it seems almost as harmless a moral nondilemma as Huck's decision not to turn in Jim. However, the play was based on a real story, and the real "Nora" was locked in an asylum by her unforgiving husband, while Ibsen's dramatization was attacked from pulpits all over Norway.

The play offers a classic structure: stasis, conflict, rising action, crisis, climax, falling action, new stasis. I have illustrated the structure with what used to be a silly example, now all too chillingly current.

The students in front of me are sitting in the same seats they sat in yesterday—not because we have assigned seats but because of force of habit. They were summoned to class by a bell and moved obediently to those seats where they are now watching the clock in anticipation of that next bell. Sitting around them are people they have known for a long time, many for years. There may be potential conflicts among the students, but unless something happens to spark a flame, chances are that life will go on.

Furthermore, they have all developed certain expectations about one another. In fact, one of the best things about going to college is the chance to start afresh without the expectations that have been accreted to them since kindergarten. In my class, the students can look around and see those they have long since pigeonholed as they themselves have been. This person is loud and assertive. That person is quiet and withdrawn.

Now, introduce a conflict. Suppose a stranger comes into the room acting strangely. Is he crazy, potentially violent? If nothing else, he is doing terrible things to our condition of stasis. Once that conflict has been introduced, we will spend a lot of time pretending things are not as bad as we think. If we can joke or ignore or dismiss the conflict, it will go away and we can go back to waiting for that class bell. Eventually, however, the tactics don't work. Someone has to make a move to resolve the situation. This moment of crisis is the moment where the conflict must be faced. This will lead quickly to a climax and a relief of the tension, but at what cost? Even if no one is injured, what will have happened to us?

Chances are, people will not all have lived up to our expectations. The class genius does not have an answer. The slow student comes up with the right ploy. The class clown cannot get beyond increasingly vapid jokes. The braggart hides behind a desk. As the action falls off after the climax, we can't go home again. Now and forever, everything has been changed: that unassigned assigned seat in that class that begins again tomorrow at the same time, that teacher I watched every day with polite disinterest, those kids I've known for ten or twelve years.

We will eventually reach a new accommodation, a new stasis, but it will take time, and it won't be in the same emotional place.

A *Doll's House* begins with lots of potential conflict (as in the Friday porch scene in *Fences* or the meal in *The Glass Menagerie*) but with conflicts that could lie dormant for ages. Then comes the letter. Nora does everything possible to keep the conflict from coming to a crisis. When she fails, we find that the real conflict is not about a fraudulent document—that is quickly resolved—but about a fraudulent relationship.

Now this, unlike the document, is a big deal in the eyes of any high school student, and all too many of them have also suffered through not only the loss of a sweetheart but also the loss of a parent to domestic dishonesty. When a new stasis is reached after the destruction of such expectations, it is definitely in a new place.

Like adult relationships, student relationships are often intolerant of the frank admission of frailty. My favorite scene in the play takes place between the secondary characters of Krogstaad and Christina. The Helmers are upstairs, where we can hear the music of the Tarantella and know what doomed, frantic posing Nora must be doing for her Torvald. Meanwhile, a new relationship is being forged downstairs, between two people who have been dishonest in the past but have learned from their failings and have learned to accept failing in other people. They take each other, warts and all, and theirs is the relationship with a chance of succeeding.

Unlike the film versions, the play must set the conversation in the Helmers' living room—because there is an elaborate "unit set" that cannot be changed for a five-minute conversation. Students who are used to me asking "tough" questions really labor to credit Ibsen with some philosophical reason for doing this, eventually settling on the obvious: "He couldn't change the set."

However, Ibsen does a pretty neat job of turning the set problem into a strength by letting the Helmers' room and the music from upstairs serve as a counterpoint to the conversation of the new lovers, a conversation taking place at the same table the Helmers will be using for their first real conversation a few hours hence.

My least favorite scene used to be the last one—at least until I saw Janet McTear's performance in the Broadway revival. This was a great object lesson in the value of live performance and reinterpretation. After we watch the endings of the two movie versions, I ask for responses and invariably the students complain that Nora's transformation is just not believable. As good as Jane Fonda and Claire Bloom are, I have to agree. Both actresses seem determined to shed the old Nora and take on the icy mantle of feminist rectitude as swiftly as possible. In this case, being so obviously right can be a real dramatic liability.

Both actresses sit their Torvald down and lecture him with strength we are even less prepared for than is Torvald—and we've been dying to stick his head in the oven since Act 1. Janet McTear was different. She began her transformation of Nora earlier. The first moment was in the scene with Doctor Rank, when Nora first teases her friend and then cuts him unmercifully. McTeer gave us a glimpse of a Nora who is even more angry with herself than she is with Doctor Rank, as if she finally sees what she has been doing all these years, playing the helpless coquette, manipulating others by inviting them to manipulate her.

From that moment, McTeer's Nora is full of looks and moans that show her preparing herself for a decision that is as terrible for her as Medea's. We really feel how invested she is in her "miracle" and how prepared she is to kill herself rather than let Torvald sacrifice himself. When this does not happen, when he proves himself to be an egotistical coward and hypocrite, she is lost, and she spends the last act groping toward a new realization of the consequences—not arriving full circle with her new suit of clothes.

Her last scene it just as triumphant, but the cost is more apparent. She clutches at her children's picture, scans the room as if seeing it for the first as well as the last time, moves back and forth from rage to bafflement to pain, the loss of everything more palpable. This is what live theater can do. I freely admit I had never seen the potential for this kind of dramatic richness in the play's ending. Students like to hear their teachers admit now and then that they have gotten it wrong.

A friend sent me something from the Internet, purporting to be an actual advice column from "Housekeeping Monthly, 13 May, 1955." It offers a "Good Wife's Guide," including the following tips for welcoming the husband home from work:

> Have dinner ready. Plan ahead, even the night before, to have a delicious meal ready, on time for his return. This is a way to let him know that you have been thinking of him and are concerned about his needs. Most men are hungry when they come home and the prospect of a good meal (especially his favorite dish) is part of the warm welcome needed.
> Prepare yourself. Take 15 minutes to rest so you'll be refreshed when he arrives. Touch up your make-up, put a ribbon in your hair and be fresh looking. He has just been with a lot of work weary people.
> Be a little gay and a little more interesting for him. His boring day may need a lift and one of your duties is to provide it.
> Clear away the clutter. Make one last trip through the main part of the house just before your husband arrives.
> Gather up schoolbooks, toys, paper, etc. and then run a dust cloth over the tables.
> Over the cooler months of the year you should prepare and light a fire for him to unwind by. Your husband will feel he has reached a haven of rest and order, and it will give you a lift too. After all, catering to his comfort will provide you with immense personal satisfaction.

Prepare the children. Take a few minutes to wash the children's hands and faces (if they are small), comb their hair and, if necessary, change their clothes. They are little treasures and he would like to see them playing the part. Minimize all noise. At the time of his arrival, eliminate all noise of the washer, dryer, or vacuum. Try to encourage the children to be quiet.

Be happy to see him.

Greet him with a warm smile and show sincerity in your desire to please him.

Listen to him. You might have a dozen important things to tell him, but the moment of his arrival is not the time. Let him talk first—remember, his topics of conversation are more important than yours.

Make the evening his. Never complain if he comes home late or goes out to dinner, or other places of entertainment without you. Instead, try to understand his world of strain and pressure and his very real need to be at home and relax.

Your goal: Try to make sure that your home is a place of peace, order, and tranquillity where your husband can renew himself in body and spirit.

Don't greet him with complaints and problems.

Don't complain if he's late for dinner or even if he stays out all night. Count this as minor compared to what he might have gone through that day.

Make him comfortable. Have him lean back in a comfortable chair or have him lie down in the bedroom. Have a cool or warm drink ready for him.

Arrange his pillow and offer to take off his shoes. Speak in a low, soothing and pleasant voice.

Don't ask him any questions about his actions or question his judgment or integrity. Remember, he is the master of the house and as such will always exercise his will with fairness and truthfulness. You have no right to question him.

A good wife always knows her place.[4]

The piece is apocryphal—this Web site lays bare its provenance—but it makes for a good laugh, particularly if the girls take turns reciting the list in fake, singsong voices. However, there was nothing funny in the fate of the woman on whom Ibsen based his Nora—her husband had her institutionalized. There is nothing funny in today's statistics about women in a lower standard of living than their husbands in their first year after divorce, while men are better off.[5]

Who is more acutely aware of this than the children of such marriages? There is one thing that strikes a universal that is sadly as telling today, even in high school, as it was in late nineteenth-century Norway. When Torvald says that he would sacrifice his life for Nora but not his honor, she looks at him for a moment and says the play's most famous line: "Millions of women have." The line drew standing ovations in late twentieth-century New York. It gets quite a reaction in class as well.[6]

Students may not be able to get a high school diploma in theater, but great plays are still there to further education.

NOTES

1. Eurypides, *Medea and Other Plays*. London: Penguin Classics, 1963.

2. e. e. cummings, "since feeling is first," in *e. e. cummings a selection of poems*. New York: Harcourt Brace and World, 1965.

3. Henrik Ibsen, *A Doll's House*, in *Four Great Plays*. New York: Bantam, 1984.

4. "Good Wife's Guide," *Housekeeping Monthly*, 1955. See Snopes.com/language/document/goodwife.asp for a discussion of the supposed "Guide," along with some bona fide and almost as disturbing advice for housewives.

5. Lenore Weitzman, *The Divorce Revolution*. New York: Simon and Schuster, 1985. This book put forward the statistics that 73 percent of women were worse off and 42 percent of men were better off in the first year after divorce. A Google search for *The Divorce Revolution*, however, will produce criticism of both Weitzman's methodology and conclusions. Other studies reduce her 73/42 disparity to more like 30/10.

6. For information on the case of Laura Kieler, the reviews of the original production, and the alternative ending Ibsen was forced to write for the German production—an ending where Nora decides to stay with Torvald after viewing her sleeping children—see http://www.ibsen.net/index.gan?id=472.

Chapter Eight

---○---

The Little Things
that Matter
Emma and *Pride and Prejudice*

In the course of our day, what makes us feel good—or bad?
What's more important, the great events in the newspaper or the
    comments in the hallway?
To what extent is all morality social morality?

IN A "GREAT BOOKS" CURRICULUM, full of "dead white men," it is a
relief to return to the very different voice of a woman. (To supple-
ment the curriculum, my students must complete a ten-page paper
on an author of their choosing, and I tempt them to try their skills
of analysis on more contemporary authors, featuring more women
and people of color. This has yielded papers on Tan, Allende,
Tyler, Hood, Morrison, Hurston, and Kingsolver, to name a few.)
Nowhere is "voice" more crucial to an understanding of an author
than in the case of Jane Austen.

    Novelist Ann Hood taught me a wonderful lesson with two short
stories by Raymond Carver, "The Bath"[1] and "A Small Good Thing."[2]
Both stories deal with a child struck by a car on his birthday and his
parents' reactions. The second story is much longer and seems to
answer a number of questions left dangling or very simply expressed
in the first. Students tend to see the second as an improved rewrite of
the first. However, they are two very different stories, reflecting two
different worldviews, and ending with two sacramental acts that take
the characters and the readers in opposite directions.

Both stories are really about how safe, pleasant worlds can crumble under threat. In the first, the parents are isolated from their world and from each other, and the story ends without our learning about the fate of the child as the parents each attempt, unsuccessfully, to retreat into the comfortable isolation of the bath. It is a kind of reverse baptism, one that might offer safety, security, and a ritual cleansing of the world's taint, without any rebirth. The child's fate is irrelevant to the story. The point has been made.

So, too, in the second story, though we learn here what happens to the child. The parents here reach out to each other and to the larger world, ending in a ritual breaking of bread (rolls, actually) with a grieving, embittered, but empathetic baker. Every detail that was left seemingly unfinished in the first story is fleshed out in the second, not as an improvement, but as a deliberately different authorial response to the material.

"The Bath" was the story originally published by Carver, but only after severe cuts by an editor who changed not only the tone of the story but also its view of the world. "A Small Good Thing" shows how the restoration of those cuts did not just make a more pleasantly "finished" story, it made a different story. Sweating the details makes all the difference in life and in literature.

Some years ago, a student confessed that she just "didn't get" Jane Austen. It was just soap opera, she said, just like Danielle Steel. I confidently insisted that Austen was vastly superior to Steel, to which the student confidently asked, "Have you ever read Danielle Steel?" I had to confess I had not. Honesty is the best policy—ask Hamlet. That weekend, I resolved to make up my deficit. I went to the library and pulled every Danielle Steel novel. The result has become a staple of my class—a dramatic reading of the best of Danielle Steel.

My hat goes off to anyone who can make a fortune writing books these days, and I subscribe to the idea that reading anything is better than reading nothing. Danielle Steel is not Jane Austen, not because she is rich and famous and people like her books. It is because her books are about plot and Austen's are about ideas. Steel's prose is purely functional, designed to develop incident, with no attention to diction or tone. Before I sound too snobbish, I submit that one cannot talk about morality in Jane Austen's world without talking about diction and tone. I submit that the world of today's high school student is much the same.

The first pages of a Steel novel (in this case, *Palomino*) will suffice. They usually begin with people "squinting," hair color is always mentioned, and something happens to render all moments either "long moments" or "short moments."

> Hurrying up the steps of the brownstone on East Sixty-third Street, Samantha squinted her eyes against the fierce wind and driving rain that was turning rapidly into sleet. It whipped her face and tingled as it pricked at her eyes. She made a soft purring noise, as though to urge herself on, and then stopped, gasping, as she fought with the lock, her key refusing to turn. Finally, finally, the door gave, and she fell into the warmth of the hall. For a long moment she just stood there shaking the dampness off her long silvery blond hair.[3]

One wouldn't call an author who turns out five-hundred-page novels with such regularity lazy, but Steel is just not about sweating the details.

In Steel's *Star*,[4] we have a seduction scene, a variation on the old "casting couch" scenario, this one taking place in a pool. Pay particular attention to the number of ellipses in the text.

> "What are you going to do with me?" She was terrified.
> "Make you a movie star." He whispered softly, but suddenly she wondered what he wanted in exchange for that. Maybe the stories about Hollywood were true, but she prayed silently that this time they wouldn't be . . . please god . . . not this time. . . .
> "I wouldn't hurt you Crystal, trust me." She nodded, unable to speak as he held her, and slowly, ever so slowly he moved closer to her and kissed her. "You're very beautiful . . . the most beautiful woman I've ever seen probably." He kissed her again and she started to cry.
> "Please . . . don't . . . please. . . ." She was shaking so violently that it touched him.
> "I'm sorry little girl. I didn't mean to frighten you. I only want you to be happy." And then, as she stared at him, he swam to the

edge, got out, and wrapped himself in the towel again, and she was open mouthed with amazement. He liked her, he admired her, he wasn't going to rape her.

Move over, Emmeline Grangerford. Jane Austen would not have written that last sentence, and not just because she would have considered the word "rape" indecorous. I stop there, not because I'm afraid of appealing to my students' prurient interests at 8:00 A.M., but because the laughter at the clichés . . . , the improbabilities . . . , and the unnecessary adverbs . . . has become so loud that other classes are being disturbed. Nevertheless, Danielle Steel will be pleased to know that many of the students confess to having read the book, and more to having seen the made-for television movie.

After Crystal suffers her fate worse than death, her true love, Spencer, calls offering to come to her rescue. "But he was in no way prepared for Crystal's words. They hit him like a wrecker's ball in his guts as he listened." In addition to important information that he was actually listening to the words as they hit him, the wrecker's ball conjures up nostalgic images of Wile E. Coyote. It seems Crystal is afraid that Ernie, her producer/gangster pool partner, will harm Spencer. To prevent this, she professes her love for Ernie.

"Have you gone crazy?"
"No," she sounded so real that it broke her heart to say the words, but better to hurt him like this than to let Ernie do it with his minions.

Hang on a second. "Minions"? Where did that come from? Here is a diction lesson for the ages. Once a few of the students admit to knowing what "minions" means, we discuss its use. Would Tony Soprano use the word? "Awright yuze guys, get da minions tagetha and meet me at da Bada Bing Club." What sense of diction puts such a word in the mind of Crystal, and on the same page with the image of her non-SAT words hitting Spencer like a wrecker's ball in the guts?

Not to worry; Steel recovers. The paragraph ends, with tears rolling down Crystal's cheeks like (I have the students complete the sentence—you guessed it) "sheets of rain."

Again, Danielle Steel is not as concerned with the niceties of language, and she really has no reason to be. Her books are satisfying reads for millions of people. The point is that Austen is doing more.

Jane Austen is also doing more—with less. I write on the board the years of Austen's life: 1775–1817. What events took place during this time? The American, French, and Industrial Revolutions, a second war with America, upheavals in the Empire and at court, the rise and fall of Napoleon. How much of it gets mentioned in Austen's novels? There are soldiers, to be sure, but they are only around to be run off with by feckless little sisters.

Austen had two brothers who fought the French and a cousin whose husband went to the guillotine.[5] Austen was certainly not unaware of larger events. Again, it has often been said that she wrote about what she knew best, and that was a small slice of society in the South of England. True as it is, this is not a very interesting explanation. There's something else to be said, however, and it is much closer to the reality of high school students.

Austen recognized that at the end of the day, happiness depends more on a few well or poorly chosen words than it does on the great events of the world. This is why her books translate so well to film, both period and modern revisions, not to mention unfortunate modern retellings of *Pride and Prejudice*, which include zombies and a vampire named Darcy.

Ask any student how his or her day went at school. If you get more than a shrug and a grunt, chances are the story will be about what a teacher or fellow student said to and about him or her. A single sneering word can ruin a day and will be remembered long after the science or history class is forgotten. The combination of words is what forms the web of relationships that has so much more to do with happiness than events in Afghanistan or Korea.

My school is close enough to New York to have had students directly affected by 9/11, but the case can still be made. Students are all too conscious that they are living history. They are every bit as aware of world events as was Austen, but, like her, they spend their lives listening. They are listening to the diction that establishes the tone in the high school hallway. Austen pays more attention to these matters than does Steel, because she has to. To convey the morality of everyday life, you have to note the details.

As an example, I show the wonderful film of *Emma*[6] and the Box Hill excursion (volume 3, chapter 7 of the novel) where Emma crafts a single clever sentence that deeply wounds a helpless older friend.

A game has been proposed: to say to Miss Woodhouse one thing very clever, two moderately clever, or three very dull indeed.

> "Oh, very well!" exclaimed Miss Bates. "Then I need not be uneasy. Three things very dull indeed. That will just do for me, you know. I shall be sure to say three dull things as soon as I open my mouth, shan't I?" [looking around with the most good humored assurance of everyone's assent] "Do you not all think I shall?"
>
> Emma could not resist.
>
> "Ah, ma'am, but there may be a difficulty. Pardon me, but you will be limited as to number—only three at once."
>
> Miss Bates, deceived by the mock ceremony of her manner, did not immediately catch her meaning; but when it burst on her, it could not anger, though a slight blush showed that it could pain her.
>
> "Ah, well—to be sure. Yes, I see what she means [turning to Mr. Knightley], and I will try to hold my tongue. I must make myself very disagreeable, or she would not have said such a thing to an old friend."[7]

The film does a fine job of showing how Emma's remark was not aimed at Miss Bates. In fact, it is the conduct of others—particularly the insufferable Mrs. Elton—that offends Emma. As is so often the case, however, one lashes out at the weakest member of the group, not the most offensive. As Emma's friend Knightley tells her later, the thing that is most offensive about her comment, the results of which are immediately apparent on the faces of all the party, is that they wounded a weaker person in front of a group, which would be guided by Emma's opinion.

This situation takes place in every hour of every day in every high school in America. These exchanges are the stuff of tears and sleepless nights. Austen renders them spot on, and she does it with her attention to language. Diction and tone *are* morality, the morality of the everyday, of the quick "snap," of the laugh you went along with, of the relief you felt that someone else got picked on instead of you.

I share a moment from my own first-grade experience. I can remember with regret every pain I have ever inflicted on another human being (more than I would like to count), but perhaps the earliest is of a cold day in the playground when I was standing alone and a boy came up to me. His nose was runny and he wore dirty clothes, but he smiled as he asked me to play with him. I said "no." I'll take to my grave the look on his face. If his parents asked him that day if he had had fun at school, his response would have been about me, not about the Cold War or the Supreme Court's recent ruling on integration.

Emma also has some timeless things to say about love, which helped make it adaptable by Hollywood for the movie *Clueless*. Emma thinks she knows enough about love to play matchmaker, with consistently disastrous results, until she realizes she is *in* love with the man who has been right there all along. Of course, the old saw is that Austen heroines learn from their mistakes and are rewarded with a good marriage. This may seem a bit dated as a worldview, but if you substitute "love" for "marriage," you can feel justifiable happiness for Emma, and Elizabeth.

Pride and Prejudice[8] brings together Austen's most famous feuding lovers in Elizabeth and Darcy. They would be perfect characters in a reality television show based on high school seniors. From its famous first sentence, the novel is full of aphorisms and clever comebacks. Is there any group that more jealously guards privileges, is more concerned with status, is more enamored of verbal facility than American teenagers?

Students can have some fun with "The Rules of Basic Etiquette" from Pool's *What Jane Austen Ate and Charles Dickens Knew*,[9] but while the rules may have changed, the impulse to establish rules has not. Neither has the need to act responsibly.

Students are quick to love Mr. Bennet's wisecracking and need to be coaxed into the idea that along with his cleverness comes a dangerous lack of concern for what will happen to his family once he has departed without a male heir. They are quick to love Elizabeth and Darcy's putdowns and must be coaxed into accepting that

Elizabeth's less clever sister, Jane, and Darcy's less clever friend, Bingley, are a good deal closer to what is necessary for a successful marriage.

Elizabeth and Darcy need to have some of the pride and prejudice (they both suffer from both) knocked out of them—he by her rejection of his proposal and she by her disastrous support of Wickham—before they can find each other. Darcy is justifiably proud of his family and Elizabeth is justifiably proud of her cleverness, but each must admit the limitations of that pride.

To see this happen, students must understand what a catastrophe Lydia's elopement with Wickham would have been in Austen's time. Nowadays it seems to students no big deal. In Austen's world, it would have precluded not only Lydia's marriage into "polite society," but also her sisters'. In short, it would have destroyed her family. This is not rebellion against a hypocritically repressive society; it is social irresponsibility, and, even worse, irresponsibility toward your loved ones. It is a good lesson for young people to learn: rebellion can feel good, but not if others have to pay for it, particularly loved ones.

Faced with the elopement, Mr. Bennet has no witticisms to offer and shows his real impotence. The ever likable Mr. Bennet has already had one of the most chilling lines in literature when he discusses Elizabeth's possible marriage to Darcy: "My child, let me not have the grief of seeing *you* unable to respect your partner in life." Typically, other people's shortcomings are griefs visited upon him, but the italicized "you" hints at a hideous admission that his marriage to Elizabeth's mother is without respect. Short of what the ghost tells Hamlet, can any father's statement be more crushing to a child's idealized hopes for love?

Faced with Lydia's elopement, he accepts blame in a pathetic statement of ineffectuality: "let me once in my life feel how much I have to blame. I am not afraid of being overpowered by the impression. It will pass soon enough."

For all her admittedly intolerable single-mindedness on the subject of marriage, is Mrs. Bennet really the frivolous one?

Elizabeth, the daughter who is most like her father, has to admit that her cleverness failed her because she was blinded by her animosity to Darcy and accepted the conniving Wickham without her usual astute judgment. Darcy has to make a herculean effort to effect a marriage between Lydia and Wickham, which will mean that the detested scoundrel Wickham will enjoy a new status—as Darcy's brother-in-law, a member of his family. Each must give up a little of the very thing that led originally to such pride, and such prejudice. However, at least they are capable of doing this, and they will be rewarded.

Again, a good marriage is Elizabeth's reward, and again it seems right, even in our modern view. It is also Darcy's reward, and the two of them are likely to make a real relationship. Those people in Austen who are too pigheaded to see or admit mistakes of judgment are doomed to remain articles of derision, such as Mrs. Elton and Lady Catherine, and our heroines' emancipation from what they represent is clearly a cause for celebration.

Austen is all about the importance of the little things, about the moral responsibility (not just social responsibility) of decency, about the limitations of status and privilege (though not their total rejection), about the acknowledgment of mistakes, and about the second chances that come to the emotionally and intellectually honest. Austen is about love. What could be more relevant to today's young people?

As with Austen, as with Carver, it is the small, good things that can make all the difference. Like the creators of fictional worlds, we all have to have the self-assurance to set a tone for our own lives and the self-respect to sweat the details in sticking to that tone.

NOTES

1. Raymond Carver, "The Bath," in *What We Talk about When We Talk about Love*. New York: Vintage, 1989.

2. Raymond Carver, "A Small Good Thing," in *Cathedral*. New York: Vintage Contemporaries, 1989.

3. Danielle Steel, *Palomino*. New York: Dell, 1985.

4. Danielle Steel, *Star*. New York: Dell, 1989.

5. Jenny Bond and Chris Sheedy, *Who the Hell Is Pansy O'Hara?* New York: Penguin, 2008.

6. *Emma*, Miramax Films, 1996.

7. Jane Austen, *Emma*. New York: Signet Classics, 1964.

8. Jane Austen, *Pride and Prejudice*. New York: Signet Classics, 2008.

9. Daniel Pool, *What Jane Austen Ate and Charles Dickens Knew*. New York: Touchstone, 1994.

Chapter Nine

―――――――――――○―――――――――――

Dealing with Loss
"The Wanderer," the Hemingway Hero,
and *The Tempest*

Why is life unfair?
When is crying not whining?
How do you lose and keep on going?
What is real courage?

"IT'S NOT FAIR" is the favorite complaint of teenagers. The typical answer from we worldly-wise adults is "Life's not fair." As facile responses go, this one is pretty much on the money and sadly appropriate. Life is not fair, but in addition to just glibly announcing this, we owe a bit of understanding. After all, it is the life we gave them.

Is it because the teenagers' complaint often comes in the form of a whine that we react so cavalierly, or is it because we do not want to admit how angry we ourselves are at the unfairness of it all? Hemingway was more empathetic.

Not all students are world weary enough to appreciate Hemingway's more subtle Lost Generation *weltschmerz* or the stoicism that must accompany it. I have had students argue that Robert Cohn is the misunderstood hero of *The Sun also Rises*, and this seems a natural enough reaction from young people who have been raised in a culture that promises the best as a birthright.

Students are more willing to accept the nobility of unrewarded sacrifice when it comes from the story of a humble fisherman like Santiago in *The Old Man and the Sea*. How can we get them to see that their own ocean is full of sharks, and that they can ennoble themselves by struggle, even if they lose their fish?

Two stories that help to bridge the gap are found in Hemingway's *Men without Women*: "In Another Country" and "Hills Like White Elephants."[1]

"In Another Country" begins with a short paragraph of simple but symbolic description—gutted animals, powdered with snow, twisting in a cold wind that comes from the mountains where the war is—often cited as one of the author's best. The story centers on a wounded American in an Italian medical rehabilitation facility. He is literally in a foreign country and is learning their deceptively simple language. However, he is urged by an Italian major to speak the language grammatically, in other words, with an appreciation for the rules, and he must learn the rules of another country—the country of bitter, life-altering experience.

The war is a metaphor for life—as it has been in works as old as *The Iliad*. Those soldiers who have been longer at the front are different from the ones who were lucky enough to be quickly wounded, even if the latter were wounded more severely.

The major has seen a great deal of the war. Formerly a fencer, he now sits in the useless rehabilitation machines without hope, knowing he cannot return to his former life. He tries a new life, however, marrying a beautiful young girl, only to have her die suddenly and unexpectedly—a casualty not of the war, but of life.

Devastated, he lashes out at the young American, who is unaware of his loss. Composing himself, he apologizes:

> "I am utterly unable to resign myself," he said and choked. And then crying, his head up, looking at nothing, carrying himself straight and soldierly, with tears on both his cheeks and biting his lips, he walked past the machines and out the door.

I ask the students to list the terrible emotions displayed by the major. How can he be crying, yet soldierly? What does it mean that he is looking at nothing? The beauty is that there is no denying his pain, or blaming it on anyone or anything. His is the human spirit utterly bereft. Is this a country we all must visit at some time?

Again I remind them of the Anglo-Saxon in "The Wanderer" and his Dark Ages awareness that friends are lent, kin are lent. I also remind them of Camus. Should this awareness lead us to despair or strengthen our resolve to cherish the term of the loan?

Another kind of loss is depicted in "Hills Like White Elephants." Told almost entirely in dialogue, the story ranks as one of the most humane, least judgmental stories on the impact of an abortion on a relationship.

The story takes place in a train station café, "between two lines of rails in the sun." The trains go in two directions, but the couple's direction is already set. What is also set, though unacknowledged by the man, is the loss of their relationship. The man says he wants only the woman. The woman looks out over the lush fields and the river to the hills beyond as a cloud comes across the picture: "And we could have all this," she said. "And we could have everything and every day we make it more impossible."

The man answers, "We can go everywhere," but the woman insists, "No, we can't. It isn't ours anymore."

The abortion is certainly a compelling issue, but in all relationships don't there come moments of choice, after which things are lost, after which things cannot go back to the way they were before? At the story's end, the woman is sitting at the table smiling at the man and insisting "There's nothing wrong with me. I feel fine." Is she being ironic, even sarcastic? Or is she, like the Major, accepting with sorrowful but soldierly resignation, that it is impossible to have a life without change—without loss?

Students need to know that great books can be funny. How could anyone love literature if it were always treated like a necessary dose of medicine or a trip to the weight room? *The Tempest* is technically a "comedy," but it has some very serious implications. Like *Twelfth Night*, it offers hilarious scenes, particularly involving Trunculo and Stephano; however, it offers some interesting insights into the nature of society.

I use *The Tempest*[2] as a controlled research assignment: students are to read the play and three essays I provide them, come up with a thesis, and use all three and only those three articles to support the thesis. This is a time-honored way to avoid the Internet-assisted term paper. The three essays neatly set out the traditional ways of seeing the play, ranging from a paean to a rustic utopia to a more cynical attack on human nature as inevitably sinister. Is society at fault for the evil men do, or is it something intrinsic in our nature? Bring in the morning paper to illustrate the point—any morning will do.

Once on the island, can all of the fighting for power, all of the machinations that lead us to hurt one another, become foolishly irrelevant? Granted that not many people want to be duke nowadays, but plenty want to feel power over a group. Is this corrupting vision really an inescapable part of any society? Even on the island, murderous usurping seems the national sport. One way to view the play is that the magic of Prospero renders all of this absurd, and that the whole crowd learns its lesson before setting sail for Milan with Prospero restored and Miranda married off.

Of course a more cynical view is that the corrupting influence of power is just as real on the island, which Prospero has taken from Caliban, and that Miranda's "oh brave new world that has such people in it" is a hopelessly naive sentiment given what we have seen of the people she is now meeting. In this view, nothing will change once that ship sails back to the cowardly old world, because people are people.

Of course there is the whole business of Prospero's being an alter ego for Shakespeare, what with the play's taking place in real time and Shakespeare's obvious ability to manipulate people with his own magic, at least within the confines of his world—or globe. The "Shakespeare's farewell to the stage" interpretation is actually very attractive to teenagers. They like neat correspondences: A equals B. Biographical criticism is easy because you just connect the dots. However, on a recent wintry night in London, I saw Derek Jacobi breathe new life into this old idea.

His Prospero was about loss. He had lost his dukedom, he was losing his power—he was losing his daughter.

His Prospero reminded me that the deposed duke was not just bidding farewell to his books. He was letting go of his daughter and viewing his own mortality as well. It was the acknowledgment of her womanhood that put one foot in the grave for the suddenly old man. He was wondering what kind of world he was leaving for his child, and what sort of judgment people would make of him.

Ask your students if they have ever thought of their own parents having such concerns. How do the students think their parents feel about them growing up? Do they think their parents worry about them? Do the students think their parents worry about their opinion of them? Do the students think their parents worry about their own mortality? Prospero was putting things right not just with an eye toward retirement. He was accepting the inevitable.

If parents are perplexed at what makes their teenagers tick, the same is true of the teenagers trying to figure out how their parents ever got to a place teenagers are confident they themselves will never reach. The thought that parents actually worry about what will happen to their children, about the legacy they will leave them, about how their children see and will see them is worth reminding teens of, now and then. Life's a tempest and then you die. However, in this comedy at least, the lessons come gently.

Every decision made involves the loss of the alternative not chosen. Every change involves the loss of the old. Loss can be painful. Is there anything in life that calls for more courage?

NOTES

1. Ernest Hemingway, *Men without Women*. Harmondsworth, England: Penguin, 1969.

2. William Shakespeare, *The Tempest*. New York: Simon and Schuster Paperbacks, 1994.

Chapter Ten

―――――○―――――

The Need to Dream

Of Mice and Men, The Glass Menagerie, and The Great Gatsby

What does happen to "a dream deferred"?
Can we live without dreams?
Are dreamers of use to our society?
Can a dream be achieved "by any means necessary"?

THESE MAY SEEM like three strange books to treat together. The real reason *Of Mice and Men*[1] is taught in eleventh grade in my school is that it is an easy book (memorable situation and only a few characters) to use for the "critical lens" question on the New York State Regents exam. There is plenty of literary stuff to discuss as well—symbolic as well as lyrical descriptions, good old foreshadowing, and a world in microcosm. Of course, Steinbeck was saying something about the need to dream, about the way a dream can humanize even the hardest person, and how the loss of dreams can harden the best heart.

It is difficult to get students in Westchester County, New York, to connect with Lennie and George's longing for a shack and some rabbits. The vision makes more sense, however, when you hear the two men talk around it, talk about the way if someone comes by and they like him they will welcome him in, but if someone comes around trying to boss them or putting on airs, they will order him off. The dream is about controlling one's destiny in basic ways that are denied to the average teenager as surely as they are denied to

91

the two tramps. Even the word "tramps" draws a chuckle today and needs explanation, but I keep the lecturing on the Great Depression to a minimum. It is not as necessary as one might think.

The shooting of Curly's dog shows the same role-playing one can find in any high school hallway. Teenagers know better than most the feeling of being confronted by a group, of feeling that one's weakness is being circled like a wounded fish surrounded by sharks. When the characters in the bunkhouse are confronted by a problem with implications for social dominance, one character is helpless. One is brutally frank. One tries to change the subject. One insists on a measure of decency. Most have nothing to say. This is a very familiar dynamic. And yes, this is a world in microcosm and the scene is a foreshadowing.

The dream itself is particularly attractive to precisely those people who are most hopeless. Crooks is excluded from the bunkhouse because of his color. Candy is dismissed because of his disability. They are sad, but no more so than the "little big man," the boss's son Curly. Every school has at least one of these. Then there is the poor woman who is known only as "Curly's wife." Her dreams of stardom are closer to those of an *American Idol* hopeful, but she is as much of a loner as Crooks or Candy. However, she stomps on Crooks when he gets so caught up in his dream that he forgets his place. Ultimately, she destroys the dream when her loneliness brings her to tease Lennie.

The sad thing, of course, is that the men had taken the first tentative steps toward realizing that dream. It was so close that they felt they could reach out and grab it, and then it was taken away. We end up back at the pond where we knew we would be from the first chapter. In that chapter, the pond was presented as a garden of Eden, with dappled shadows, golden light, and animals living in harmony. George's decision to shoot Lennie causes much debate in the classroom. Even more interesting, however, is the students' understanding of what the act costs George.

Whenever George started to tell Lennie the dream, he always began with how the dream they shared made them different from all the guys who wandered the land with no one "to give a god damn" about them. When George shoots Lennie, he kills a part of himself. All those times the exasperated George was forced to recite the details of the dream, he was reinforcing it in his own mind as well as Lennie's. Lennie was the connection to the dream, and without him George will not be able to recapture it and will become just another hardened laborer. He and Slim go for a drink, and the last word is left for Carlson, who doesn't see what the trouble is.

Of Mice and Men is a simple, great read, and it stays with students well past the Regents test, because it warns them to hold on to a dream. The alternative is the crusty wound described by Langston Hughes.

I begin *Hamlet* with my AP students by asking them to make a list of their own attributes and those of the adult world. They usually describe themselves as honest, as caring, as inquisitive. They describe the adult world as phony, cold, closed. They will say they are afraid of it. When I ask what they are most afraid of, one girl said, "I'm afraid that when I get there I'll become like all the adults I know."

In the harsh world of the Depression, in the sad life on the ranch, childish, hulking Lennie had protected George from the day he would have to become like all the others. If only their dreams could protect our children from becoming like the worst of us; we can only wish them longer life and more happiness than Steinbeck gave Lennie and George.

Nobody gets shot in *The Glass Menagerie*,[2] but it may be an even more frightening read. It posits a world where only certain dreams are allowed, and where dreamers themselves are an endangered species.

It is still the time of the Great Depression, but we are now in an inner-city slum. We are also in the memory of the narrator, a strange device for a play. The fact that the narrator is dressed as a merchant mariner tells us that this is not going to be a play about whether he can escape from his cramped apartment. He warns us, however, that this play is about illusions, and that dreams are harder to escape from than any apartment or family.

The play opens with the usual condition of stasis, with Tom joining his sister and mother at the dinner table. The scene is full of tension, but it is a scene that could be repeated indefinitely were it not for Laura's failure at business college. In Scene 1, however, the lid is kept on the long-simmering family issues by the possibility that Laura will succeed, make a life for herself, and allow Tom the freedom to leave without guilt.

In my classes we act out the first scene—the three characters fit neatly in front of the class—and I introduce the theater idea of "purpose phrase,"[3] asking the class to write down a verb phrase that captures what each character wants in the scene. For Tom we arrive at some version of "to escape," even if only to the fire escape for a cigarette. For Laura it is "to keep the peace," changing the subject to avoid friction. For Amanda it might be "to keep up her dignity," with a forced gentility that can only further alienate Tom. These needs are the driving force throughout the play.

Students are often quick to choose sides, deciding that Amanda is a monster, Tom a hero of liberation, and Laura too pathetic to believe. Particularly when they see parts of the play acted out, they have to learn to modify the easy assessments. Amanda has not had an easy life, and she will do anything for her children, including telemarketing and demonstrating brassieres in a department store—activities hardly in keeping with her vision of Blue Mountain. Tom is genuinely repentant after he insults her, and there are moments of real tenderness and understanding between them.

When we learn Laura's full story, she seems just as sad but more believable. The play offers a useful lesson in tolerance: not the usual lesson in racial or religious terms, but tolerance in the family, seeing parents and siblings as complete human beings rather than only in their roles.

With the news from Rubicam's, again acted out in front of the room by two students, we begin the cat-and-mouse game of avoiding the real issues. The students have to direct one another, milking for all they are worth scenes like the announcement from Rubicam's, the "El Diablo" monologue of Tom, the makeup scene with Amanda, the announcement of the gentleman caller. The scenes are all masterful presentations of what a character wants and the varied tactics he or she will use to get it.

After the scenes are acted out, we watch scenes from two different filmed versions, one with Katharine Hepburn, Sam Waterston, and Michael Moriarty (absolutely the best gentleman caller I've ever seen), and the other with Joanne Woodward and John Malkovich.[4] The scene where Amanda tells Laura about her past and tries to get Laura to answer the door for Tom and Jim offers two completely different choices by the respective Amandas. I have several pairings act out the scene and then show the two film versions.

Joanne Woodward's purpose phrase emerges as something like "to relive the dream," standing alone across the room, lost in a reverie over jonquils (a jonquil, by the way, is a form of the narcissus—how appropriate?), and imperiously demanding that Laura march to the door. Katharine Hepburn's choice is more "to share the dream," as she embraces Laura, paints word pictures for her, and dances her around the room. She helps Laura rise from the sofa and ushers her partway to the door. The interesting thing is to see how theater allows two great actors to make completely different choices with the same text.

Neither choice is bad. The only bad choice is no choice, the kind of hollow, toneless desecration of the text one gets from reading the play aloud as the students sit at their desks. Once again, in truly examining what the characters want from one another and for one another, the students are forced to abandon the easy images of insensitive parents and victimized offspring.

Even the apparent throwaway conversation between Tom and Jim on the fire escape is a wonderful example of the drama that comes from mutually exclusive "wants." I play a game I call "dream endings" to help the students find each character's purpose. The student has to imagine how his Tom or Jim would like the scene to end if he could rewrite Tennessee Williams.

If Jim could do this, Tom would say something to the effect of, "Jim, you're so right. I'm tearing up this merchant marine union card and taking a night school course in public speaking. The yearbook was right. I can see you're heading for great things. I just hope I can measure up." Likewise, if Tom could rewrite the scene, Jim would be dropping out of school, telling Mr. Mendoza where he can put his shoes, and heading for the nearest pier, all the while thanking Tom for helping him see the light.

Each person really wants the other to validate the choices he has already made.

We talk about such "advice" scenes, so common in students' junior and senior years, as they plot their courses, debate their choices, and hear the advice of counselors and parents. There are several of these scenes in the play *Voices from the High School*. How much are such scenes really designed to help the other person and how much is designed to make the adviser feel good about himself?

Of course, Jim finds a more receptive audience in Laura. Only by acting out the scene and by seeing it acted out can students appreciate the subtle magic Jim works on Laura, using his very real charm to bring her out, only to dash her hopes. A good actor can also portray just enough of the sincere huckster in Jim, as he describes the wonders of technology, education, money, and power, "the cycle that democracy's based on." Jim has a dream and it is classically American. He worships technology and dreams of prosperity. Education is utterly utilitarian, designed to get him in on the ground floor of the new television industry.

It is almost too perfect, but with the right actor, very believable. In contrast, Tom dreams of movie adventure, Amanda of dead gentleman callers, and Laura cannot exist outside the beautiful but fragile world of her glass menagerie. "Unicorns, aren't they extinct in the modern world?" asks Jim.

Of course unicorns are creatures of myth, though perhaps Jim's vision of modernity will indeed make even myth extinct. He does kill Laura's unicorn, knocking it from the table as he swings her in her first dance. However, Laura is not devastated. She is almost relieved that the unicorn, and she herself, may now be "normal," like all the other horses. (Surely, her earlier description of how she was stared at for her deformed leg rings true with any high school student.) Even when she finds out he is engaged, she is not prostrated on the couch, and she finds the strength to give him the now "normal" horse as a souvenir.

It is only when he has left her alone with Mother that she retreats to the phonograph, and Amanda calls her an unmarried cripple with no job. It is at this point that Tom realizes the situation is hopeless.

When Tom resumes his place on the fire escape to finish his narration, we assume things did not go well for his sister (Williams's own sister was institutionalized) and that his guilt has prevented him from ever really making good on an escape to a world of care-free adventure. The last moment, with mother and daughter blowing out their romantic candles in a world now lit by lightning, is terribly sad and touching.

Of course, the first Hollywood rendering of the play could not deal with this ending. In that version, Jim has no fiancée to meet, and he and Laura are left looking out the window at a world of new possibility. I encourage my students to talk about what has happened to make the ending of the play really the only acceptable ending, and we talk about the necessity of dreams.

Surely a society needs Jims. Jim is the kind of person who helped build twentieth-century America. A society full of Toms and Lauras is not going to find a cure for cancer. It is not going to defeat Hitler. Tom and Laura are dreamers, but not doers. The American dream is only validated by action. The question is whether a society needs Toms and Lauras almost as much as it does Jims, if it is to keep its moral compass, its heart, its sense of a bigger picture.

The same vision (some would argue it was the only one Williams ever had) becomes even more ominous in *A Streetcar Named Desire*.[5] Stanley Kowalski is the gentleman caller on steroids. Gone is the affability and innocence, replaced with the ultimate perversion of American utilitarianism. Stanley, like Willie Loman, thinks it is better to have knowledgeable acquaintances than to have knowledge. Like the desiccated Chillingworth, the powerful Stanley sins against the human heart.

If Blanche is all that is old—romantic, outdated, anachronistic in the true sense, corrupt and gone to seed—Stanley's crushing, careless modernity is clearly the greater evil to Williams. Stanley is capable of bringing forth new life, even in the infertile ground of the DuBois family. However, his judgmental insistence on honesty, on light, is ultimately cruel, self-interested, and hypocritical. After his rape of Blanche, which drives her to madness, he has to resort to a lie.

Students are quick to condemn Blanche, who has done everything wrong, who is weak and deluded, who is clearly capable of lies. It is a testament to Williams's skill that he manages to convert the teenagers. By the play's end, they see her as the victim, and they accept her insistence that she only lied to make the world prettier than it was. A lodestone is the character of Mitch. Is he better off for knowing the truth about Blanche? In some ways, yes he is. However, he doesn't think so. He surely is not grateful to Stanley.

Is Stanley's vision of modern America, so much harsher than that of the well-intentioned Jim, true today? Are the dreams that allow the fragile to survive not to be valued? If only those dreams that add to power and utility are to be nurtured, will we ever get beyond the caveman caricature of Stanley from the first scene, as he throws a hunk of meat at his pregnant wife?

This issue of the right kind of dreams is very much a part of *The Great Gatsby*.[6] I have students read the book while we are acting out *The Glass Menagerie* and take time out from the play several times a week in order to do some guided reading with an emphasis on characterization, imagery, and tone. When we finish with Jim and the Wingfields, we are ready to tackle Gatsby.

Again we have an outsider to usher us into the strange world of Gatsby. Nick does not immediately take to his neighbor, but Gatsby comes to be seen as great not only due to his excess and flamboyance but also because of the way he stands out in contrast to Tom Buchanan, Jordan Baker, and the Wilsons.

Tom is a racist, a hypocrite, and a brute. He rails against Gatsby, but keeps a mistress whose nose he smashes. He has no compunction about setting Gatsby up to be murdered. He is also rich enough to know that someone else will tidy up his messes for him. My own school is economically diverse enough that this characterization is not lost on my students. The rich are different from the rest of us.

Jordan Baker is an amoral opportunist who cheats even at games. She is not as obviously bad as Tom, but the cheating rings a bell. If she will cheat at golf, she cannot be trusted with a person's feelings.

The Wilsons are pathetic, she with her aristocratic airs and he with his full name proudly proclaiming him "proprietor" of his shabby repair shop, and whose dreams of going west will ultimately die with his wife.

Next to people such as these, Gatsby's underworld connections seem less egregious, given his generosity of spirit and his "capacity for wonder."

Nick realizes that Gatsby was better than any of them. In the wasteland dominated by the images of ash heaps and an oculist's billboard, Gatsby is the embodiment of the American ability to dream. The fact that his dream is as ephemeral as any daisy is not the point. We cannot judge Gatsby on the quality or attractiveness of his dream, any more than we can demean George and Lennie's rabbits or Laura's glass menagerie.

Like the knights who sought the grail, the power of the dream is in what one is willing to endure for it. Gatsby remakes himself, a very American ideal, and earns (steals?) money not for its own sake but as the key to enter a closed world. He never understands that no amount of money can buy him the sense of entitlement possessed by the Buchanans who have known wealth all their lives.

Teenagers can understand these issues. How are the rich still different from you and me? How much of the rich person's world can be bought by the newly wealthy music, sports, or movie star? What are the subtle differences that the very rich guard jealously while pretending they do not exist? Can we not admire the purity of vision that causes the poor boy to devote himself to anything—music, sports, entertainment—that will help him achieve the ultimate prize, whatever that prize may be?

And what of the young people? Have they retained some capacity for wonder? As they fill out their college applications and make their first plans for the takeover of the world, do their dreams go beyond Jim's, or are they just looking no further than the ground floor of the cycle democracy is based on? What is it in this world they are inheriting that can still offer them the same vista that the "breast of the new world" offered those Dutch sailors?

If nothing, will they be left standing on the shore, looking at the green light that recedes before them? In a modern world that offers them tawdry fantasies, but where unicorns are extinct, will they be left like George, Tom, and Nick to marvel at a time or at persons who once offered a chance for something more?

NOTES

1. John Steinbeck, *Of Mice and Men*. New York: Penguin, 1993.

2. Tennessee Williams, *The Glass Menagerie*. New York: New Directions Books, 1999.

3. I first observed this and other phrases and exercises in workshops taught by a number of talented theater teachers and professionals at the Educational Theater Association Annual Convention in Cincinnati and at the Summer Director's Course at the Yale School of Drama.

4. The best film versions of *The Glass Menagerie* for comparison are Broadway Theater Archive, 1973, and MCA/Universal, 1987.

5. Tennessee Williams, *A Streetcar Named Desire*. New York: Signet, 1974.

6. F. Scott Fitzgerald, *The Great Gatsby*. New York: Scribner, 1995.

Chapter Eleven

─────────○─────────

The Weight of the Past
Oedipus and The Piano Lesson

Can we write our own destiny?
How much does the past shape the future?

EVEN IF FROST'S "DESIGN" does not keep us awake at night, even if
Pilate's bag of bones does not break our backs, we still must wonder
at times if our upbringing has shaped us. You do not have to be a
Freudian psychologist to wonder.

Sophocles' Thebes would seem to be a long way from our world,
but it would seem to offer an unforgiving moral climate in which
there is little room for ambiguity or chance for heroism. Then there
is the students' response to the basic plot.

Despite the constant bombardment of sexual imagery to which
teenagers are subjected, they are pretty conservative when it comes
to their own parents. The thought of their parents engaging in any
more than one act of procreation is something they do not want to
contemplate. Incest is something beyond the pale. In *Song of Solomon*, Macon Dead's accusations about his wife's conduct with her
own father are so luridly effective that students discount Macon's
self-interest and Ruth's denial.

In *Oedipus Rex*,[1] the fact that the students already know what
Oedipus did and are revolted by it actually helps to give them an
approximation of the Greek audience's experience.

I remind them that when they read *Romeo and Juliet* they all knew it would end badly, and yet no matter how often one reads or sees the play, one wants to boot that friar's donkey (or get a thinner friar) to get that letter to Romeo, all the while knowing that he will not get that letter and will not know that Juliet is just napping. The ancient Greeks likewise knew going in many of the stories behind their plays. They went to the theater as part of a religious ritual, expecting not a surprise ending, but a confrontation with the *ti deinon*, the terrible, in a manner that sparked philosophical contemplation and purged difficult emotions.

The whole notion of catharsis is easy for teenagers to understand. Consider the typical slasher movie. Everyone can tell in the first five minutes of the movie exactly which teenagers in the little world in microcosm are going to get axed, impaled, or immolated. The students have great fun with this observation and can offer fifty examples. Why then go to these movies?

I mention that Alfred Hitchcock was once asked if the secret of good horror was not knowing what was going to happen. He said it was precisely the opposite. The audience knows what is going to happen; they just do not know when and how. Crucially, they also know they are powerless to stop it. It is that anticipation that keeps them on the edge of their seats. However, this is only part of the issue. What is going on in addition to a cheap thrill? How do the students feel after their two hours in the dark of the multiplex? The answer is that it feels good to be scared, and even better to emerge into the afternoon sun afterward.

Make a list of the things that are facing a typical teenager about to enter the adult world. In addition to general teenage angst, they have to worry about a fragile economy and the chance that their lifestyle won't be even as good as that of the previous generation.

They worry about getting into a college, about paying for that college even with enormous student loans, about paying back those student loans if a good job does not materialize upon graduation. They have to worry about problems we adults have not solved and have even made worse: global warming, terrorism, war, AIDS, ecological and technological disasters, racism, sexism, overpopulation, the division between rich and poor.

What is the chance of our teenagers solving one of these issues next Saturday afternoon? However, in the darkened theater, they can subject themselves to a terror they can put a face on—or at least a hockey mask. They can watch that terror emerge, and they can watch it run its course. They can invest in that terror all their own unexpressed terror at the real issues that stare them in the face from their television screens. They can do what they cannot do in school—they can express fear. They can scream with their friends to their heart's content.

All the while they know the fictional creation cannot really hurt them, that it will be over in two hours, and that it will be dealt with by the surviving teenagers—often with minimal adult help—leaving only the possibility of a sequel next year. That is catharsis. No wonder they go to these movies.

Of course, the Greeks also intended a moral lesson in their confrontation with the terrible. The terrible was not a psychopathic murderer as much as a hero (or heroine) faced with a moral quandary of horrific implication. Welcome to Thebes.

Oedipus Rex opens with a plague and a king's admirable, if somewhat self-important, decision to shoulder the responsibility of freeing his people from their affliction. I remind the students that the plays were presented as part of a religious festival, and I show them a wonderful Janus production of a filmed play that emphasizes the use of masks, stylized gesture, and choral speaking. At first, they howl at the production, but they eventually buy into the ritualized storytelling that emphasizes not the facial expression or intonation of an individual, modern actor, but rather the importance of the words themselves and the questions they pose.

The play is a model for dramatic irony, for the effect on the audience of knowing what the characters do not know, of wishing things could work out differently, of knowing that they cannot. Oedipus is justifiably proud of having solved the riddle of the sphinx and having saved Thebes, but he has come to count too much on his intellect.

How appropriate for a high school senior—or for any human being. Do we not prize our intellect as the thing that separates us from other life-forms, and that separates us from one another as we get our college admission packages? Oedipus constantly cries for knowledge, and as surely as Adam and Eve did, he will regret it once it is his. The knowledge he will gain is of the horror of ultimate taboo and of the consequence of thinking he can escape the fate of the oracle by outsmarting the gods.

Oedipus's heroism, however, comes in his acceptance of fate. In the course of the few hours the play takes to bring his horror to light, Oedipus's past failings become virtues. He was rash in his killing of Laius, and still more rash in his accusations against Creon; however, when he begins to realize the enormity of the evil he has wrought, he does not hold back. His rashness is transformed into heroic determination to see the events through to their inevitable end and to sacrifice himself to save the city.

Like a Hemingway hero, he does not whine about fate—and if ever someone had cause to whine it is Oedipus—nor does he offer extenuating arguments. Like a Bigger Thomas or Meursault as much as a Hamlet or Beowulf, he accepts his fate, even embraces it, blinding and banishing himself. There's no hint of "it's not fair" even in Oedipus's final moments in Thebes. No "Twinkie defense" here, only heroic integrity in the face of a horrible fate, the insistence that we cannot change who we are, but can act bravely in the face of life, accepting the consequences of our actions.

A play that offers an opportunity to ask similar questions is August Wilson's *The Piano Lesson*.[2] Two siblings war over what to do with a piano. The piano was purchased in a slave owner's exchange for two of their own family members. It was then decorated with the carved history of the family throughout its bondage. It was finally stolen at the cost of a father's horrible death.

The son, Boy Willie, wishes to sell the piano to purchase the land his ancestors had worked as slaves. Boy Willie has been offered one of Wilson's favorite Faustian bargains (see *Ma Rainey's Black Bottom* and *Seven Guitars*). A white man is purchasing unique musical instruments throughout the black neighborhood.

He is buying up the "song" of the people, their spiritual birthright, and they must sacrifice that music if they wish to "move ahead" in the dominant culture.

Boy Willie's sister, Berniece, wishes to keep the piano, but more out of fear and anger at the pain it represents. In the climax of the play, a minister fails to purge the house of the spirit of the last member of the slave-owning family. Berniece succeeds, however, by appealing to the ghosts of the piano, the empowering spirits of her long-suffering family.

Unlike *Oedipus*, this is a play full of humor and eventually triumphant humanity. Like Sophocles, however, Wilson is asking whether we remain bound by the limitations of our past, if that past is indeed a measure of our fate. Oedipus's horrible past proves inescapable, but it leads him to a heroism that he did not exhibit in his former arrogance. Berniece's horrible past proves embraceable and leads her to a power she did not exhibit in her former bitterness.

Berniece's past includes a family captured and enslaved, a family divided, a father killed, a husband killed, a mother bereft. Yet she can ultimately see through the awfulness to the strength it has taken to endure all this and keep moving forward.

Have students interview their elderly relatives for empowering stories. One of my students found an elderly aunt who spoke to her for the first time about riding in the back of the bus, not in Mississippi, but in affluent Westchester County, New York. Another spoke to a longtime teacher on the verge of retirement who made the student realize that the mall where the students congregated was built on the remains of a black neighborhood that had been bulldozed, like August Wilson's, for urban renewal. I shared the fact that my own great grandparents came from Ireland because my great grandfather was Protestant and my great grandmother was Catholic and they were unable to marry in their homeland.

It is good to remind students that their elderly family and neighbors are a rich source of history. It is even more important that they learn that personal history—Berniece's, Milkman's, their own—is a rich source of pride and empowerment.

NOTES

1. Sophocles, *Oedipus Rex*, in *The Oedipus Cycle*. New York: Harvest Book/Harcourt, 1949.

2. August Wilson, *The Piano Lesson*. New York: Penguin, Plume Book, 1990.

Chapter Twelve

---○---

Private Morality
and Second Chances
The Scarlet Letter, The Crucible,
and *The Kite Runner*

Which sins are worse than others?
How do we find forgiveness?
Does life give second chances?

WHAT DO *The Scarlet Letter*[1] and *The Crucible*[2] have in common, other than stern faces beneath comical black hats? Both books are about morality, hardly a surprise given the setting in Puritan New England. What comes as a surprise to students, convinced as they are that the novel is nothing but a sadistic, Ichabod Crane English teacher's idea of fun and that the play is nothing but an aging hippie social studies teacher's idea of allegory, is that both books are about the redemptive power of love in a land founded on a belief in second chances.

I do not require my students to read "The Customs House" section of *The Scarlet Letter*, but an image from that section is certainly appropriate for this chapter. Hawthorne imagines himself rebuked by the spirits of his Puritan forebears. "What is he? A writer of storybooks!" says one, "What kind of a business in life—what mode of glorifying gods, or being serviceable to mankind in his day and generation—may that be? Why, the degenerate fellow might as well have been a fiddler!"

Reading storybooks? What mode of glorifying the gods of educational orthodoxy, or of being serviceable in imparting basic skills

107

uniformly assessed that will give us quantifiable data and will give the business world competent and pliant workers, may that be? Students assume next I will be wanting them to find room in their new four-by-four block remediation schedule for art and music.

Back to the love stories.

In *The Great Gatsby* we saw a vision of the first Dutch sailors finding in now overgrown Long Island, the fresh green breast of a new world, something, perhaps the last thing, that could truly match man's capacity for wonder.

In the first chapter of *The Scarlet Letter*, we see the past where Gatsby's current would draw us. It is a past where, whatever the "green light," despite "whatever Utopia of human virtue and happiness" they sought, the first English sailors who founded Massachusetts deemed it immediately necessary to built a jail.

And what of today? Is America still as sternly moralistic? I show the students a political cartoon from a British newspaper, with Bill Clinton standing before a tribunal of Puritan fathers, being given his scarlet letter across a table covered by an American flag.[3] I mention Europeans' perplexity at the Lewinsky scandal. We examine the rhetoric of political speeches from the left and right. Commentator Bill Maher, for example, opines that while Canada and Europe are moving away from religion and are becoming more humanistic, Americans seem to be going in the opposite direction.

Students are split on the importance of real religious observance in our public lives. They are quick to point out their disgust, however, with whatever smacks of religiosity, particularly when it is practiced by the venal or corrupt—the *Canterbury Tales* variety. Surprisingly, they are also split on the role of popular culture as an alternative to religious orthodoxy. The gyrations of MTV are "just a show," not a real statement. I recall telling my own father that the now hopelessly tame lyrics of the 1960s love songs were not a clarion call to moral degeneracy but "just songs." As frightening as what I hear from car stereos today may seem, teenagers still seem to think they are "just songs."

So, are we a more judgmental society? Is a typical high school a judgmental society? What happens to those who go against the judgment not only of the administration but also the more potent judgment of their peers? How ready are we for "a tale of human frailty and sorrow"?

Five women and a man speak outside the jail door before Hester emerges. Let six different students read the lines as if they were presented in a play and then discuss the effect. Why are the women more judgmental than the man? Why is the young woman the most understanding? Why does one woman insist that Hester "has brought shame upon us all"? Who else is mentioned besides Hester? The answer to the last question is, of course, Dimmesdale.

The little exchange becomes so clear when presented dramatically. What is the role of law? If it is a code of community values, how is it decided? Is there a danger or a strength in arriving at such codes based on the moral dictates of a specific religion? I share with the students a recent article about modern American courts employing "Scarlet Letter Sentencing."[4] I also point out that adultery was a criminal offense, punishable by jail time, in the State of New York, until the 1960s.

What do the women gain by stating their opinions, how do they reassure themselves, what are they asserting? To what extent are we making an object lesson of others in order to prevent bad behavior? To what extent are these judgments designed to reassure us of the rightness of our own behavior? These same questions are debated in criminal law classes. Some offenses (rape, murder) are *malem in se*—bad because they are intrinsically bad. Some things (tax evasion) are *malem prohibitem*—bad only because we say so.

Hester Prynne has had a child out of wedlock and refuses to name the father. Against whom has she sinned? Why is it important that her sin be acknowledged and punished?

It is important to modern readers that we accept that Hester herself believes she has done something wrong. Once again, the great book doesn't allow easy answers. This is not just the heroic individual against the repressive society. Hester has done something we may or may not find sinful, but which we must agree is unfortunate. Furthermore, in the world of this novel and in the heart of this character, we have to accept that she believes it was sinful. The question is, where does she go from there? This is a tougher question than a mere assessment of blame.

Of course, there are others to blame. Students are justifiably quick to point out that there is a man involved, though they must wait a few pages to find that there are two. Again, there are no easy answers. Students are quick to realize who the real father is, and they are easily contemptuous of the minister's speech in chapter 3; however, they soon come to see that Dimmesdale is less of a hypocrite than they first thought and is acutely aware of his sin and of his continuing cowardice.

Appropriately, before we delve into the heart of the minister, we meet the man who will become his nemesis. Hester's husband, long missing among the Indians and given up for dead, is no cardboard villain. Chillingworth vows no vengeance against the wife he should never have married, and his explanation of why he married her is truly touching. His vengeance against the yet unknown man "who has sinned against us both" will consume him, however, just as Dimmesdale's half-spoken guilt will consume him. Only the publicly humiliated Hester will endure.

Why does Hester stay? When she is beset by an unforgiving community and Dimmesdale is aware of the evil machinations of his physician, why do they not head west into that fresh green breast of the new world? They meet in the forest and are unable to go farther. The forest is established from the start as the place where the devil lives. What does this mean? What was literally outside the settlement? Indians, wild animals, most of all, the unknown. What was not outside the settlement? The comfort of like-minded people, the rule of law. Of course, we have seen the limitations of that comfort and that rule, but how easy is it to do without them?

Teenagers are quick to say they want to be free of society's oppression, starting with the school administration's rules against wearing hats and carrying cell phones and leaving the campus for a better lunch than that offered in the cafeteria. Are we just as quick to demand liberation from the school's rules against bullying and harassment? What do we gain from society? What can we not do without? Most important, how much of our individualism are we willing to trade for the best of what society has to offer?

In the theocratic world of the Puritans, the insecurity of a life outside the community might be expressed in a belief that the forest is the land of the Dark Man. However, isn't the fear of the unknown something we all share? Hester might be forced to live on the outskirts of the village, but her address is still Boston, Massachusetts. Dimmesdale might feel the daily weight of the community adulation carving an "A" into his chest, but he has no identity outside that community, beyond his ordained role as its minister.

The second page of the novel mentions Ann Hutchinson. Here in Westchester, there is a river, and, more important for my students, a highway named for her. Ann Hutchinson was thrown out of the Massachusetts colony for her religious beliefs, the Puritans having come here not for freedom of religion but for the freedom to practice their own religion. The Puritans were isolated in a strange and hostile land, and perhaps their insistence on conformity can be understood as we look at what has happened to our own pluralistic society in the aftermath of 9/11.[5]

Hutchinson moved first to Rhode Island and then to New York. She was befriended by the local Indians, who were, unfortunately, being brutalized by the Dutch, the descendants of F. Scott Fitzgerald's first sailors who were now colonizing the area with a vengeance. The Indians warned Hutchinson that war was coming and that, though their quarrel was not with her, she would be in danger. She stayed and was killed with her whole family. Why did she stay? The Indians could not have understood why she could not go back where she came from, to Rhode Island or Massachusetts or England.

Can we understand why, with the North American continent lying to her west, she could not move any farther into isolation and uncertainty?

Hester and Dimmesdale and Chillingworth must stay within their society and must make their decisions, as we all must, within the circumscription of social conventions and community attachments. There is no easy escape from the compromises, the trade-offs,

that we all must make by virtue of our conflicting desires to be free
and to belong.

This is the ultimate problem with rejection of society. It's not
only that some of society's rules are necessary, it's that our desire
to be a part of something bigger than ourselves is inescapable. As
any teenager who ever decided to wear his baseball hat backward
or decided to chuckle at a hurtful joke knows, we need the group
though we sometimes choke under its oppression.

All groups have laws, not just governments and school admin-
istrations, and the more one wants to be a part of that group, the
more one is confronted, even in America, land of opportunity, with
the issue of compromise. All three characters are alienated *from*
their society, although only Hester is alienated *by* her society.

The final scene on the scaffold could only take place with the
redemptive power of love.

Of the three sinners, Chillingworth's awareness of evil leads him
to greater evil, to a single-minded obsession with vengeance. Dimmesdale cannot allow himself to look anywhere but within his own
flawed heart and cannot accept the power of forgiveness until the
final moments. Hester, however, has experienced the full personal
consequence of sin as an unwed, single parent, without family other
than the child she must support (the strangest child this side of Stephen King) and ostracized by her community. However, the exposure
that has caused her such pain leads her to an understanding neither
man has and leads her ultimately to a profound compassion for others, which will be her salvation both in this life and the next.

Hester weakens momentarily when she plans an escape by ship
for her and Dimmesdale. On the morning of her trip, appropriately
Election Day, she finds to her despair that Chillingworth has somehow discovered her plot and booked passage on the same ship. She
realizes there is no escape as she and her child wait at the foot of
the scaffold. When Dimmesdale emerges from the church and sees
them there, his last strength and their literal support help him take
his place above the crowd, where some say his bared breast shows
a livid A in the flesh over his heart.

Cheated by the minister's public admission, Chillingworth soon
dies. Having driven everything from his life except vengeance, he

has nothing to sustain him. Again, however, the mark of a good book is its acknowledgment of rounded humanity, and Chillingworth, in death, does one last good deed, leaving his fortune to Pearl, allowing her to be free. Hester, who leaves for a time, decides to come back to her home, to the place that anyone would associate with pain and shame. She outlives the memory of her sin and establishes such a reputation for charity and goodness that younger people assume the A stand for "Able," perhaps even for "Angel."

As Dimmesdale noted in the forest, "We are not, Hester, the worst sinners in the world." Chillingworth's revenge makes him worse than even "the polluted priest" because "He has violated, in cold blood, the sanctity of the human heart." Hawthorne teaches us that there are sins against the law, against the social order. However, there are private sins that may escape even the harshest media eye, but that wound in the most profound way. Of all the things that are *malem in se*, perhaps this is the greatest—the sin against the human heart.

Hawthorne was so concerned with the consequences of sin and guilt, even across generations, that he changed his family name, adding a "w" to avoid association with ancestors more sinister than the one in the Customs House who chided him for writing story-books. One was a judge in the most infamous of American trials, the Salem Witch Trial, and he is a character in Arthur Miller's *The Crucible*, a play that, like *The Scarlet Letter*, is about public and private guilt, about sins against the human heart, about community, about love.

If it has been the fate of *The Scarlet Letter* to be dismissed as too hard and too irrelevant, it has been the fate of *The Crucible* to have its relevance easily assumed for all the wrong reasons. Of course the play is an important statement against naming names and scapegoating, but to today's students the anticommunist fervor of the 1950s seems as current a history lesson as the War of 1812.

The play can only stand on its own universality. It is certainly born from the author's concern for the direction of his country's democratic experiment, but it is at its heart not about an establishment conspiracy to deflect community anxiety at a politically expedient target. At its heart as a drama it is the story of a husband and wife: a husband painfully aware that it is his sin that precipitates the trials, and a wife who feels herself too plain to trust love—and whose first attempts at forgiveness would "freeze beer." The play is about their struggle to find their goodness in their love.

We discuss the Red Scare. Paul Robeson was attacked on a road in Peekskill, and books were banned in neighboring Scarsdale.[6] I also share a harrowing account of current witch hunts in Nigeria.[7] I tell them of the playwright Arthur Miller's experience, his appearance before the House Un-American Activities Committee, and the threat of the blacklist.

I also show them some real trading cards called "The Red Menace," which kids of my era collected like baseball or Davey Crockett cards.[8] The images are crude, depicting scenes like "Police State," "Fleeing the Reds," "Berlin Kidnapping," and "Visit by the Red Police." The cards proclaimed a "Children's Crusade Against Communism" and urged us to "Fight the Red Menace." I show them the cards because the newspaper articles of the time only show the foolishness of the Red Scare, but none of its widespread popularity and pervasive influence.

I ask them why Miller wrote a play about the Salem Witch Trials rather than the McCarthy hearings. Eventually, the reason becomes clear.

Miller presents us with an indisputable piece of hysteria that had become a source of shame even by Hawthorne's day. When we see people trying in vain to prove that they are not witches, see them accused of murderous evil for either the slightest of nonconformist sentiments or simply for the self-interest of others, see them offered the calculated bargain of their own lives for the lives of their friends, we cannot help but be driven to fury at such injustice. Had Miller written an overt attack on the Red Scare, a sizable portion of Americans simply would not have agreed with him.

I ask students who may find this unlikely to consider our own post-9/11 world, our preoccupation with homeland security, the necessary support for our "commander-in-chief" and his decisions. The threat of the communist menace was strong enough in my day to have children taught to cower under their desks in case of nuclear attack in much the same way we now have regular fire drills. The threat of terrorism is strong enough today—to do what?

Of course, the play also works as a larger indictment of scapegoating, a subject every teenager is familiar with.

A Yale School of Drama production of *The Crucible* began with a lengthy improvisation, an abridged version of which I do with my class. It went as follows. Pretend you are living in England, in a village where your family has lived for generations. Your house is several hundred years old. If you step out your front door and look to the left and right, you see much the same vista your grandfather saw. The stone wall turns to the left as it has for centuries and leads up the hill toward a cluster of houses and an ancient church.

One day a rider from London arrives with dire news. You and your community are to be required to worship God in a manner prescribed by the king. The community holds a meeting and it is decided, after debating options, that there is no choice but the most terrible—they must leave for the newly discovered lands across the Atlantic. What things—only the most obviously utilitarian—can you take with you? What will you have to leave behind? Imagine that you can take only one personal item: a portrait, a single book. What will it be? Imagine the day you walk out of your door and leave it ajar, looking up and down the stone-lined lane for the last time in your life. You cast a last look inside before you and your family head for the port. There you board the ship.

Imagine the conditions in the North Atlantic crossing. You and your neighbors are farmers, not sailors, and you are crammed belowdecks as the ship tosses. You have no privacy, your food is terrible, your sanitary conditions nearly nonexistent. At long last you see land. You go ashore, give thanks, and begin to build. You chop down the dense stand of trees, feeling the weight of the ax. You lift rock after rock, stump after stump from the fields that are so unlike those you left behind. Beyond the clearing is the forest, a vast unknown. Are there savages, strange animals watching you as you work?

You build your own cabin, but you also build a communal space, a meetinghouse, for your reason in being here is to worship, and that belief is what defines your community. One night, a stranger knocks on the stockade gate. He comes from another village (it seems a late student is always heaven sent at this moment, so he can be sat in the middle of the crowd) that has suffered calamity. He asks to come in and be one of you. Given all you have gone through, do you let him in?

Hold a meeting such as the community might have had and consider the questions that they may have asked. What is his trade? (A carpenter we can use. A poet, no thanks.) What will he contribute? Importantly, what are his religious beliefs? Can he be one of us? He passes the test and the community lets him in. A year passes. The crops in the community have failed, and the fields they worked so hard to clear are barren. The children have contracted some strange illness, rendering them weak and listless. What do the community members do? As they meet, some may consider a rational approach. What have they done wrong? Is there something they need to change to adapt to this new world?

To the majority, driven by fear that they will lose all they hold dear after they have already sacrificed so much, there is another approach. All of this has happened since the new person arrived. What does he say? What explanation does he offer? From the middle of the room, he hears the irrationality in the voices of his new neighbors, and he offers the only explanation that will appeal to them—he offers them the name of someone else and plants the seed of distrust.

A student teacher of mine put together his own classroom activity. He simply announced that someone in the class was a witch and handed out bits of paper to each student, warning them that the paper could say "citizen" or "witch." Find the witch. Listen to the arguments, the "evidence." Before long, everyone is under suspicion. Of course, when all the students reveal their scraps of paper, none of them says "witch."

So, the play is not simply topical to the 1950s, but is also topical to our present political climate. It is also universal as a statement against the larger irrationality of scapegoating, of finding blame rather than solutions. It is, however, also a personal drama, and personal drama needs to be about something more personal than political allegory.

Miller wrote the screenplay for the most recent film version of his play. It is quite wonderful, unlike the most recent film version of *The Scarlet Letter*, to which Hawthorne was unable to contribute. The Miller film includes some new scenes that work well and includes the additional forest scene he wrote for stage production, but which is now usually relegated to the appendix and never produced.

It is no surprise that the role that won the Academy Award nod was that of Goody Proctor.[9] While Abigail has center stage in the courthouse, her minx is rather one-dimensional compared to the half of marriage represented by Goody Proctor. The strain of Scene 2, with its mix of pride and fear and hurt and guilt, with its movement from her bland stew to her husband's futile attempt at her defense, is a frighteningly real portrayal of a relationship in trouble.

Anyone can appreciate the scene who has ever found passion replaced by that "walking on egg shells" feeling, when one seems powerless to cure what ails the relationship, guilty over one's own failure, angered at the partner's apparent inability to solve the problem or even meet it halfway. Behind the maddening stupidity of Herrick and the cowardice of Reverend Hale lies a pair of very keen personal guilts.

As events spin out of control, Proctor cannot help but know that it is his adultery that has precipitated them. Without his sin, his weakness, the harmless "sportin" in the woods would never have gone so disastrously awry with Abigail's request for a murder charm. The girls would not have gone into their trances. Abigail would not have had to invent their story to save herself.

At the same time, Goody Proctor, soft spoken but judgmental, knows that it takes a cold heart to "prompt lechery," and that her own weakness is at least in part a spur to her husband's unfaithfulness. Of course, they are both far more scrupulous than most would be. They will both have to forgive themselves as well as each other. They will have to grant themselves their "goodness." Like the relationship of Krogstaad and Christina in *A Doll's House*, the most realistic and durable of unions are born of honesty and acceptance, imperfect unions of fallible human beings.

The courtroom scene is masterfully constructed and begs to be acted out in class. The film version is also good. Even the interplay of the judges works best when they are differentiated as individuals in their own special torments.

Hale goes from the confident expert on witches, reveling in his celebrity, to the "broken minister," urging others to lie in order to lessen his own real sense of guilt. Hathorne (minus the "w") is a hack, with just enough intelligence to be crafty, but not enough moral sense or wisdom to vary from his course once it is set. Danforth is far worse because he is smart enough to look beyond expediency and see the truth. He simply cannot allow himself to do this, but he more than any was capable of doing the right thing.

In the end, Proctor does the right thing—or does he? He wants his life once his wife convinces him that he has his goodness. He confesses, but then will not name others, and ultimately will not give up "his name." Students are torn by his decision, many of them saying they would not die for the principle of the thing. Hale insists to Goody Proctor that God is angrier at the one who throws away the gift of life than he would be at one who lies to save it. She thinks this must be the devil's argument.

Students are not so quick to agree. Could they live with the shame in a world that was then so small? Remember that there was no escape from Salem for Hester and Dimmesdale. Remember also that there was no escape for Tom Wingate in sailing around the world.

In the novel and the play, Dimmesdale and Proctor are guilty of adultery and must skirt for a time around the public shame of their betrayals. Each is helped by the woman he loves. Each ends up on the scaffold. Neither is guilty of that worst of all sins—the sin against the human heart. Both the novel and the play are puritanical in this sense: they demand hard choices, they brook no half measures.

Righteousness is not to be found in either book, neither in any public orthodoxy nor in any private judgment devoid of understanding and compassion. The choice of goodness brings pain. Even the knights of the round table knew this much, that goodness chosen for other than its own reward was no goodness at all. In both of these works, however, the alternative to the right choice is the death of the spirit.

A novel about contemporary Afghanistan might seem an un-likely companion piece, but *The Kite Runner*,[10] from its first chapter and the injunction "It is time to be good again," brings the questions of sins and redemptive acts clearly into the present. The novel also brings them into a vividly realized world we think we know but do not. Afghanistan has certainly loomed large in our awareness the past few years, but the many newspaper accounts could hardly have prepared us for the middle-class lives of Amir and his family in the pre-Taliban era.

The book takes its title from a child's game; however, like the metaphoric kite in Frost's "Design," the irony is that a child's plaything could harbor a vastly more sinister truth. The game itself is a test of manhood and a vicious one at that. The particular kite runner of the title is Amir's childhood companion and half-brother Hassan. Hassan's devotion to Amir will lead him into a Kabul al-leyway where he is sexually assaulted. That same dead-end alleyway presents Amir with a test he fails. Fearing a gang of bullies, he does not go to Hassan's aid.

The class can debate what Amir should have done. Was it possible for him to save Hassan? Would he only have endured the same fate? Does life sometimes present us with a situation such as this, only to present us with no real alternatives to guilty impotence? Later, unable to face Hassan, Amir engineers a false accusation against him, which causes the brutalized boy to be ban-ished from Amir's household, but hardly from his memory and his conscience.

Years later he has the chance, and the obligation, to leave a comfortable life in America and to return to the scene of the crimes—a Kabul now run by the Taliban. The resulting adventures will thrill most readers, thought some of the connections strain credulity. Too late to rescue Hassan, Amir must endure hardships, fear, and a terrible beating at the hands of Hassan's old assailant in order to free a child who is really Amir's nephew.

The family background to all this offers its own lessons in moral ambiguity and emotional honesty. Amir was never able to live up to his father's expectations, but his father was also never able to tell Amir the truth about Hassan's parentage. Their belated reconciliation is achieved in the setting of their diminished lifestyles in America and is connected to their attempts to preserve some sense of social and moral dignity in new roles in an alien culture.

Many of my students are familiar with this same balancing act. Even in the country now associated with the murderously puritanical Taliban, the essential sins of the novel are as much sins of omission as commission. Amir cannot face his failure to act in that alleyway. For a modern high schooler, isn't this more often than not the case? The basically good but somewhat weak person does not commit sinful acts—perhaps out of morality, but perhaps out of fear. However, that person must endure guilt for what he failed to do—again out of fear.

All three of these books, rooted in societies famed for their moral rigidity, essentially revolve around the choices made in the context of relationships. As in the family of Polonius, truth and falsehood begin not in the law books, not even in the holy books, but in the home.

NOTES

1. Nathaniel Hawthorne, *The Scarlet Letter*. New York: Signet Classics, 1999.

2. Arthur Miller, *The Crucible*. New York: Penguin, 1976.

3. Syndicated political cartoon "And when did you last see your scruples?" by Dave Brown. First published by *The Independent*, July 9, 2003.

4. Molly McDonagh, "Scarlet Letter Sentencing," *ABA Journal*, January 1, 2007.

5. Tom Tomorrow (a.k.a. Dan Perkins), "Are you a real American?" syndicated cartoon, *New York Times* Sunday Week in Review section, July 1, 2002.

6. Robert Merchant, "Hunt for Red Influence Jolted Northern Suburbs," *Journal News*, July 15, 2000.

7. Tracy McVeigh, "Children Are Targets of Nigerian Witch Hunt," *Observer*, December 9, 2007.

8. Copyright 1951, Bowman Gum, Inc., Philadelphia, Pennsylvania. The copyright note on the cards proudly adds "USA."

9. *The Crucible*, Twentieth Century Fox, 1997. Academy Award is a registered trademark and service mark of the Academy of Motion Picture Sciences.

10. Khaled Hosseini, *The Kite Runner*. New York: Riverhead Books, 2003.

Chapter Thirteen

———○———

Throwing the
Good Away

Macbeth, Fences, and *Death of a Salesman*

What makes something tragic?
Does an evil act make a person evil?
Are there "circumstances beyond our control"?

WHICH EVENT CONSTITUTES a tragedy, and which is merely pathetic?
Choice A: A respected educator leaves the building, his head full
of thoughts of Shakespeare, and is run over by a school bus. Choice
B: A respected educator leaves the building in handcuffs, along
with his impounded computer, after being caught in the district
attorney's sting campaign against kiddy pornographers. Students invariably rank choice B as pathetic, but only because kiddy pornographers are pathetic in the modern sense of the word. This launches
us into the discussion of the three plays that are the subject of this
chapter.

Recently after my class had finished reading *Macbeth*[1] we
debated the definition of tragedy. One student said the following:
"Tragedy is when you throw the good away." This may not be as
exhaustive a definition as Hamlet's discussion of tragic flaw (in Act
1, Scene 4), but it is very good.

Macbeth is a play students still warm to because it has witches,
complete with brew kettle and false prophecies—and because it is
not *Julius Caesar*. We do all the accepted activities from the Folger
guides[2]: we improv, we trade Shakespearean insults, we examine

key lines before we hit the text. We look at my model of the Globe Theater and I show them a stage manager's book from a real production. But the story is central, and the story is about a good man, described in the second scene as noble, loyal, and heroic.

Of course we have already seen the witches and know that this means some evil is primed. Acting out a scene in front of the class is helpful at replicating Shakespeare's Globe Theater staging. The witches spend Scene 1 center stage, and when they leave to meet Macbeth, every good Elizabethan knows it can only mean that the title character has the seeds of evil in him. In the next scene the king and captain meet and trade stories of Macbeth's nobility on the exact spot just vacated by the witches. Dramatic irony is visual as well as verbal.

Macbeth wrestles with his conscience, unlike his famous wife. When he falls, he really takes a tumble, but his fall comes only after we have seen a good person tear himself apart and then consciously choose to do evil.

Of course none of my students wants to be king (or queen) of Scotland. The question, however, is what one is willing to do. We explore some pertinent questions: Do you want to get into Yale, win the homecoming queen election, get a new car, or cut a CD? If you could realize your dream and you only had to do one really bad thing, one thing that went against your better nature, would you do it? If not, why not?

"If it were done, when 'tis done," if you could know that there would never be any consequence you didn't want, if you could know that no one would ever find out, would you do it? To what extent are we held back from doing evil because we fear being caught? To what extent are we moral because we want to be? This is a very real question, and it gets the students' attention.

Students truly enjoy working out the witches' prophecies, but I also point out an early, rather offhand story the witches share, about the woman who refused to share her chestnuts. The offended witch says the woman's husband is a sea captain, and she promises to send him a wind that will keep him sleepless and tempest tossed for days. She'll spin him around—until he sinks himself. The crucial point here, and one that would have brought a nod of recognition from Shakespeare's audience, is that the devil can't make us do anything.

The witches cannot make Macbeth kill anyone, do anything he is not disposed to do. It is not until their second meeting that the witches see Macbeth and say "Something wicked this way comes." In their first meeting, he is still blameless, even noble, but he has within him the seed of ambition. The witches cannot sink him, but they know he can sink himself if they keep him sleepless and tossed in a tempest of doubt and temptation. It takes most of Act 1 for Macbeth to sink himself. When he does, we can do what Aristotle wanted.

We can learn from a fall that was not the result of the devil, Twinkies, malpractice, or missing warning labels. We can be instructed in the moral consequence of immoral action. We can take our own fear of moral failure—and even the most cynical or the most sanctimonious have that fear—and we can invest it in the tragic figure. We can feel the catharsis that can only come from believing in the reality of his struggle.

In Roman Polanski's very modern (post-Manson murder) view of the play,[3] with Malcolm newly crowned, his brother Donaldbain ends up crossing the heath and meeting the witches. Polanski rewrites Shakespeare to make corruption inevitable and unavoidable no matter what the makeup of the man. Nothing could be further from the Elizabethan view. Shakespeare's tragedies are tragedies in the real sense. Without choice, without a real possibility for the right decision, there is no tragedy, and there is nothing to be learned from the play. We need to see the person who is bigger than we are take that fall, and we have to ask ourselves what keeps us, lesser mortals, from doing the same.

In Fences,[4] we see that the person bigger than we are might be a flawed garbageman. Students feel they have died and gone to heaven when reading Troy's speeches in the first scene. Once again we have stasis. The king holds court on the back steps of his proud though shabby home. He talks with the usual crowd about the usual things and with the usual emotional dynamic. However, we see the potential for conflict with Troy's job, his sons, his brother, his wife.

Named for a city famed for its heroic but ultimately doomed struggle for survival, Troy will eventually defeat himself, completing his fence only to find himself alone behind it. Troy drives his wife away with his affair, losing his mistress and being forced to ask his wife to take care of the child he has fathered. This leads to one of the great moments in the play. Troy also drives his son Cory away, having been denied his own chance to play major league baseball because of the color barrier and now convinced that his son should learn a trade rather than play college football.

Here we see the most insidious effect of racism, and it can be seen most vividly in a school: Troy has been taught by a life of racial oppression to limit his own worldview, to cut his own dreams and those of his son down to manageable size. How many of our students have experienced the same? How much has our school system been responsible? We see him in the end, sitting alone on the porch, the support of the Friday ritual now gone. Soon after, he is dead, though not before we can see—in his final confrontation with his son—that he is a better man than his father.

As my students read the play in the front of the room, I write on the board a chronology of Troy's life, and as each new piece is added to the puzzle of his missing years, we add it to the list. What emerges is a life of hardship, of victory, even celebrity, of missed chances, of bitterness, and ultimate loss. What we see, however, is that each generation can build on what it receives from the previous generation. Troy's father was a horrible man, but he did teach him the need for responsibility for one's family. Troy himself is a wounded man who inflicts pain on his family but who stops short of attacking his son as his own father had attacked him.

In the original theater production, after Troy's death, one feels a palpable loss as the figure of James Earl Jones is gone from center stage. The play ends with the preparations for Troy's funeral. At first, his son Cory, returning from the marines, refuses to go to the funeral. His mother upbraids him, insisting that his father meant more good than harm. Surely if she can forgive Troy, so can he, and so can we.

We then see Troy's last child, the child of his affair, sitting with Cory and singing a song they had each learned from Troy, as he had from his father. These two wounded offspring take Troy's place on that same back porch, in a beautiful dramatic moment that can only be realized if the students reading the parts are positioned in the front of the room.

Through the play, even when we talk of racial oppression, even when we talk of Troy's diminished options—his great speech about "bunting," for example—we never lose sight of his stature as a hero. One of the first things we hear about Troy is that he has taken on the white boss, appropriately named Mr. Rand (the currency of apartheid South Africa), over the issue of hiring colored drivers in 1957.

Troy is fighting the good fight. However, the fight has taken its toll. His taste of greatness—immediately circumscribed by society—has left him bitter. That bitterness poisons his relationship with his son. His longing to live larger—which leads him into a doomed affair—poisons his relationship with his wife. His desire to take care of his own, including the child of that affair, forces him to abandon his brother. At the end, he is as alone as Macbeth.

Troy is a killer, an ex-con, a home-run hero, a larger-than-life figure, even as a trash hauler. It is clear that he, and Wilson, and everyone in the theater see his greatness in his power to endure as well as enthrall and see his failures in his own poor decisions, his own tragic flaws.

Willie Loman—again the name is as significant as Troy's—presents a different case. In a way, the plays are very similar. *Death of a Salesman*⁵ is another indictment of the misapplication of the American dream. However, like *The Great Gatsby*, it is also another glorification of the dreamer without regard to the tawdriness of the dream. Like *Fences*, it is another story of the dynamic between father and son. What it is not is a tragedy.

The most painful moments are those that revolve around Willie's relationship with Biff and with his wife. The fact that Biff confronts the evidence of his father's infidelity in a hotel room makes its revelation just as damaging as the news Hamlet gets from his father's ghost. The scene in the restaurant is ineffably sad. However, the end result of *Salesman* is similar to that of *Of Mice and Men*.

We are left touched by unforgettable moments, but we are not filled with the "there but for the grace of God and my better decision making go I" that one feels after Sophocles or Shakespeare—or Wilson. There is nothing great about Willie as there is about Gatsby, and there is just as little self-realization. If anything, the tragedy is not Willie's so much as it is America's.

The funeral scene is particularly telling in this regard. Willie does not die brandishing a baseball bat and taking on Mr. Death. He kills himself in the mistaken belief that it will help his family. Unlike Troy, physically replaced at center stage by the real interaction between his children, we have the forced statements of Willie's brother that "Nobody dast blame that man." We feel for Willie as we did for Lennie and George, and we leave the theater questioning why our world has to produce such men only to crush them in a maelstrom of circumscribed options and empty dreams. "It comes with the territory" in a nation that still likes to call itself a land of dreams.

NOTES

1. William Shakespeare, *Macbeth*. New York: Washington Square Press, 1992.

2. Peggy O'Brien et al. (eds.), *Shakespeare Set Free: Teaching Romeo and Juliet, Macbeth, and A Midsummer Night's Dream*. New York: Washington Square Press, 1993.

3. Roman Polanski, *Macbeth* RCA/Columbia, 1971.

4. August Wilson, *Fences*. New York: Penguin, Plume, 1986.

5. Arthur Miller, *Death of a Salesman*. New York: Viking Press, 1963.

Chapter Fourteen

────────○────────

Love, Actually

Twelfth Night, Othello, and *Wuthering Heights*

Can love be too passionate?

What should one be willing to do for love?

What is the difference between love and obsession?

ROMEO AND JULIET, five dead; *Julius Caesar*, three dead, not counting soldiers; *Macbeth*, nine dead, not counting servants; *Hamlet*, six dead, not counting Rosencrantz and Guildenstern. You get all this with ancient plots, inverted sentence structure, and iambic pentameter. Such are the joys of Shakespeare. No wonder typical high school students approach Shakespeare as they would bitter medicine or a trip to Grandma's.

It also does not do much good to insist that there are funny bits in all of Shakespeare's plays. Hamlet's explaining to Claudius "how a king can go a progress through the guts of a beggar" and his put-downs of Rosencrantz and Guildenstern are great stuff, but few high school students can understand them without the help of the teacher or a footnote. We seldom get much of a belly laugh from a joke when it has to be explained. Even in Branagh's film, the grave digger scene, with Billy Crystal, and Osric's challenge, with Robin Williams, leave students with smiles of anticipation under uncomprehending eyes.

In short, the plays chosen for study in high school leave a high school student thinking Shakespeare was about as funny as a high school teacher.

With so many skills to master and so many standardized tests to cram for in order to prove mastery, it is difficult to convince the powers that be that a high school education should include a balanced appreciation for the greatest writer in the history of English. What I will argue instead is that acting out some Shakespearean comedy can provide some fresh enjoyment of real literature and provide some fresh insights into real teenage problems.

No Shakespearean comedy reads better than *Twelfth Night.*[1] Its language is fairly simple, its scenes are short, its comic situations are broad and obvious, and there are lots of insults that do not take a dictionary to grasp. What is a real surprise, however, is that Shakespeare is still talking about the same things he was in *Hamlet*.

Once again, chaos ensues when people pretend to be what they are not. A girl has to pretend to be a guy and is employed by another guy to woo a girl who falls in love with him/her, while he/she falls in love with her employer, the rejected suitor. Then his/her twin brother shows up. After much complication, order will be restored.

The old line is that in tragedies this takes place through death, and in comedies through marriage. Even specific situations echo the tragedies. Sir Toby's gulling of Sir Andrew mirrors the more sinister machinations of Iago toward Roderigo, while Orsino's arguments against Olivia's extended mourning for her brother are identical theologically to Claudius's arguments against Hamlet's mourning. It is interesting to note how much context rules the difference between something funny and something evil, something fair and something foul.

What makes the play so much fun in class is actually positioning students "onstage," in front of the class. I always admonish students to pay attention to who is onstage and remain silent. An audience will watch an actor watching someone else talk. This is lost in having students "read plays aloud from their seats."

The classic scene to illustrate this is Malvolio's "discovery" of Maria's forged letter. The students who are hiding behind the hedge (remember what happened to Polonius) cannot help but act out their fury and derision at Malvolio's self-important comments.

They use the language as only a starting place. The students fall all over each other trying to get at Malvolio.

Students see immediately that Shakespeare was adept at giving his actors situations that allowed them to play at their roles for full comic effect. The same is true of the drunken revelry of Sir Toby Belch, of Malvolio's exorcism, of the duel to which poor Aguecheek is prompted, of the final reuniting of the brother and sister. Here are the welcome themes of the holier-than-thou authority figure made fool and of the familiar scrambling of relationships (he likes her, but she likes him, but he likes her), with the additional twist of the gender-bending. And it really is funny.

A Midsummer's Night's Dream[2] gives us similar confusion of the bewitched lovers, as well as Bottom and his rude mechanicals. The play used to be taught in my school to all eighth graders, along with the magnificent *To Kill a Mockingbird*. At my school, and at how many others, both books have now been dropped in favor of more relevant curriculum, courtesy of consultants.

I used to explain the confusing parts of the four lovers using my daughters' collection of Barbie and Ken dolls. There is real emotional business, however, in the "boy who loves the girl who loves the other boy who loves the other girl" that has caused no little amount of heartache in every high school. In the comedy of Bottom, we see some slapstick with Titania, but when all is said and done, poor Bottom is left wondering at the dream he dimly remembers. He is the poor, dorky, fat kid left dreamy eyed at the suggestion that the class beauty might actually "like" him.

Pyramus and Thisbe are a fitting ending, performed with disastrous sincerity by Bottom's players. "What fools these mortals be," says Puck. Is love always a midsummer's dream, "too flattering sweet to be substantial," as Romeo mused? Is it merely the gentlest of those dreams we hold to in a cruel world?

And what does *Twelfth Night* tell us about love? "If music be the food of love, play on," moons the often witless Orsino. Why does Viola fall in love with him? Olivia seems to fall in love with Cesario, a.k.a. Viola, because the supposed servant makes fun of her rather than saying nice things to her. She later marries Sebastian simply because he is a male version of Viola, even though she's hardly had a conversation with him. Orsino marries Viola after all his doting on Olivia and after banishing her a few minutes before. Sir Toby marries Maria because she was so clever in getting Malvolio to act like a fool—by making the fool think someone actually loved him.

The comedies might present a goofy look at love, but the tragedies present something genuinely scary. *Hamlet* is so rich with ideas, with dramatic touches and with language so worthy of relishing, that it can keep students engaged for weeks—once they have seen themselves in the young prince of Denmark. *Othello*[3] is a tougher sell, because, like Shakespeare's other tragic heroes, he is getting on in years. One also runs the risk of seeing him as an inarticulate dummy, easily taken in. (See the very funny vignette in *Voices from the High School*.[4]) This is all the more of a problem because he is black. Did racism prevent Shakespeare from giving him any great speeches? Why doesn't Shakespeare let him manipulate events as Hamlet does?

Without ascribing to Shakespeare any less of a racist (or anti-Semitic in *The Merchant of Venice*) attitude than was the norm for his day, there is a way to approach the character. Witness the many recent modern *Othello* adaptations, showing the black man lionized for a particular skill (a policeman in a recent British film, a basketball player in an American), but ultimately denied a real place in society once that skill is no longer needed. In addition, however, the play's more universal theme is insecurity in love, and it is presented against a worldview much more modern and cynical than that of Hamlet.

Where Hamlet is coming upon the world's cruelty as a young idealist, Othello has seen everything. Works as different as Hemingway's "In Another Country" and Bob Dylan's "Shelter from the Storm" present the character who has already suffered great loss and invests his remaining emotional capital (Fitzgerald's famous term) in a relationship, only to lose that, too, through death or betrayal.

I ask students to consider the life Othello has already endured. Of noble birth, he is stolen from his home and forced to work as a galley slave. He then fights his way through the ranks to become a general. In short, he has suffered through a life that would have killed off Hamlet before the prince of Denmark could have made it to his sophomore year.

In fact, Othello is the antithesis of Hamlet, and not only because he is black. Where Hamlet is the "rose and fair expectancy of the state," Othello is an outsider, enjoying a fragile tolerance by virtue of his usefulness. The two men come at the same fundamental horror of people pretending to be what they are not, but they come at it from opposite directions. Hamlet is dealing with the first crushing disappointment with the adult world, but Othello has fought through many layers of betrayal long before the play begins.

When it comes to language, Hamlet himself is mightily sick of his own verbiage by the play's end, and for simple sincerity, who can top Othello's explanation of his love for Desdemona: "She loved me for the dangers I had passed, and I loved her that she did pity them."

For the first time in his life, someone has shown an interest in Othello as a person, and he dares to trust. For the first time in how many years, he dares to lower his guard. This may seem to be a gamble more suited to the person of middle age, but it is actually one that any teenager can appreciate. Just what does it take to let yourself fall in love? How much can one safely invest in another person?

The ending of the play can be discussed not in an attempt to justify Othello's supposed stupidity or Shakespeare's supposedly racist purpose, but as a truly frightening suggestion that love does not conquer all, that to love "not wisely but too well" can be destructive, even deadly. Shakespeare's famous concluding restoration of order is much less convincing here than it was in *Romeo and Juliet* or even *Hamlet*. Iago is still alive and will not answer any questions. Evil is still alive, and we have no idea why love should have been allowed to destroy itself.

Every high school student knows that "who has chosen to date whom" is very important and very public business. Every high school student knows as well that relationships are about an intensely private search for acceptance and affirmation. The more rejected one feels by the world—for whatever reason—the more one needs what

Frost called a person to govern one's loneliness. The more rejected one has felt, however, the more depleted the reserves of hope and trust that one needs.

Othello is a hero to every high school student because he is willing to fight, and also because he is willing to take the plunge. His tragedy is not that he does not have words—it is that the world has used up so much of his hope and trust. When Othello invests what is left in Desdemona, Iago sees the chance to exploit his former friend's vulnerability. The world, then as now, is a place where only the courageous look for love.

A very different, nineteenth-century voice can be heard in the Yorkshire dialect of Emily Brontë.[5] If they can get beyond the Yorkshire moors business and the fact that one of literature's most famous love stories is told to us third hand, by a tenant who is listening to a housekeeper who was present for all the great events, they will find themselves back in *Othello* country.

In this place, the polite, predictable web of social interaction and assumption—that supports more than it confines in Jane Austen—is almost nonexistent. In what was for the English reader of the 1840s a still wild land, rules fly out the window, elemental passions can be expressed, and terrible choices must be made.

A problem students sometimes have with *Wuthering Heights* is in mistakenly seeing Catherine's choice of Linton over Heathcliff as a choice of wealth over poverty. Conditioned by popular culture, they are quick to see the easy morality of such choices: the poor are deserving victims, the rich are corrupt leeches. Cast any argument in terms of rich and poor and you cannot go wrong. You also cannot strike too close to home.

Catherine's choice is between the bad boy who moves her soul and the nice guy who offers not wealth as much as sensitivity and concern. This choice has achieved the status of mythology in the high school. Get the boys wondering which category they fall into and the girls wondering which type they would choose, or have chosen.

Of course, Heathcliff is the great-grandfather of all soap opera villain/heroes. Sonny of *General Hospital* is a favorite with my daughters, but every soap opera has one. This leading man is a handsome, dark-haired man of clouded origins and ill-gotten wealth and power, with an element of danger about him. However, he also has his flashes of generosity and style, which make him seem tamable, if only the right woman could help with the rough edges. His morality is his own code of personal honor, not an adherence to any set of rules. However, within his code, he is fiercely loyal, even devoted to the people and things that matter to him, even as he is capable of lashing out without concern for norms of decent conduct.

Is Heathcliff the boy that girls long for and Edgar the one they marry? Edgar is the one parents would approve of. He will drive carefully and have their daughter home by eleven, and will not profess too much disappointment when she says they should "just stay friends." What is more, he does not do this because he is cowed by authority or because he is a simpering milquetoast, but because he really feels it is right. He is a good listener, who wants to give her all the good things. However, in the terms of today's high school, he's just a little too "soft."

Wuthering Heights makes the comparisons between Heathcliff and Edgar palpable in the descriptions of the two homes: Wuthering Heights and Thrushcross Grange. Again, it is not about money. Catherine's family is as well off as Edgar's, at least while her father is alive. The Heights are just that: a stone fortress on a cliff, baring its face to the storms.

Thrushcross Grange (even the name falls trippingly from the tongue with or without an English accent) is a genteel but sheltered place. Put it on the cliff next to Wuthering Heights and the pieces would be in Scotland by nightfall. Put the Lintons' little yapping fur ball of a lapdog in amid the hounds and it would not see dinner, it would become dinner.

For all the Heights' primitive vitality, however, there is something attractive in a place where people talk instead of shout, where the servants do not stalk around like Frankenstein's Igor, and where the plates and cutlery stay on the table and off the walls.

Heathcliff is the wild life force that attracts the vibrant Cathy, but a little Linton is nice now and then. As Cathy grows to womanhood and needs to think about a place in the world beyond the

Heights, the need for what the Lintons represent becomes more acute. Is a girl's Heathcliff just a juvenile dream that has to be put aside with other childish things?

Cathy hits the nail on the head when she says to Mrs. Dean that a marriage to Heathcliff would debase her, but that a life without him is unthinkable. Of course, the driving moment of the novel comes halfway through that statement, when Heathcliff runs away, never hearing the second half, and not returning until Linton has won Cathy away from him—at least in the eyes of God and the law.

When Heathcliff does return, he is no longer the swarthy but endearing servant boy. He is now as demented, destructive, and amoral as Ahab. He is still attractive, even to Linton's sister, but when he fathers a child, the boy has none of the good qualities of either side of the family. Heathcliff's treatment of Isabella and Hareton and his kidnapping of Cathy's child to marry his own revolting boy are inexcusable evils, but they are born of a great passion. Is Cathy in part responsible for this for having rejected that passion for a life with Edgar?

A third location in the novel is the moors, those Hound of the Baskerville wastelands that separate the Heights and the Grange. When they are young, Cathy and Heathcliff find joy there, because it is a place free from rules and free from decisions. In the mature world, however, the very lack of definition, that wild untamed nature of the place, is what allows bad things to happen. It is there that Heathcliff kidnaps Cathy's child, and it is there that Cathy's ghost resides. In life, she juggled what the two houses represented. In death, she must remain outside. Just ask our poor narrator.

Of course, Lockwood is the quintessential outsider, like the visiting engineer in *Ethan Frome*. He comes from another, more civilized part of the country—the part, coincidentally, where the bulk of Brontë's readers would have resided. The story grabs him, and those readers, when Cathy's icy hand seizes his. He then must be ushered gradually into the wild world of Yorkshire by the all-knowing Mrs. Dean.

He is then able to witness with real understanding the denouement of the story, as Cathy's child and Hareton will form the union

Cathy and Heathcliff could not, and as Cathy finds herself in death with her two men, one on either side. (In a final sneer at rules, Heathcliff bribes the sexton to remove the side panels from his coffin and Cathy's while Edgar remains in his own box.)

This was always the answer to the riddle: Cathy needed both men. A life without passion is insipid. A life without rules is chaos. It is a balancing act that all people who wish to be part of a society must undertake. "Take your passion and make it happen" might be a cute song lyric, but as a prescription for life, is it useful? Unlike the rich-versus-poor issue, this is a tough question for the teenager to ponder.

NOTES

1. William Shakespeare, *Twelfth Night, or What You Will*. New York: Washington Square Press, 1993.
2. William Shakespeare, *A Midsummer Night's Dream*. New York: Washington Square Press, 1958.
3. William Shakespeare, *Othello*. New York: Washington Square Press, 1993.
4. Peter Dee, *Voices from the High School*. Boston: Baker's Plays, 1982.
5. Emily Brontë, *Wuthering Heights*. New York: Signet Classics, 1959.

Chapter Fifteen

---◯---

Some Great Deed
The Iliad

How do we leave our mark in the world?
Why do we need pride?
Can we have too much?
What is the value of moderation?

THE ILIAD[1] IS SEEN as even more unapproachable than *The Odyssey*. There are no adventures, no fantastic creatures, no single compelling storyline about a man returning home. It is just a clanky war story about a hero who spends much of his time brooding like a spoiled brat and about battles that seem repetitious and always end with some god tilting the tables away from the deserving. We never get to the one thing everyone remembers about the Trojan War—the horse business. We do not even find out who wins.

Of course *The Iliad* is about so much more. For one thing, just look at the relationships. Did Homer leave anyone out? There are friends, lovers, siblings, husband and wife, parent and child, commander and subordinate, god and man.

There are also some problems to sort through that hit awfully close to home for teenagers. With recent graduates now in Afghanistan and Iraq, students are once again forced to ask if something is worth dying for. Even if there were no real war with which to contend, the concept of warfare—emotional as well as physical—as a metaphor for life, is not strange to the high school student. Most of all, the question of how we prove our individual significance as people is certainly of interest in a world where assaults on self-esteem are as ready to hand as the missed foul shot, the broken date, or the college rejection.

Of course, *The Iliad* is a war story. Even skipping the list of the ships at the end of Book II, the set pieces, however, seem to follow a pattern. A Greek squares off against a Trojan and gives a speech: I am so-and-so, the son of so-and-so who distinguished himself in the fight against those other guys, and I am well liked in my lovely village of such-and-such where they grow the best olives you ever tasted. The Trojan then gives as good as he has got, before the two fight a while until one god or another decides to pay attention and someone ends up with his head lolling like the head of a poppy, falling to the earth.

As repetitive as these fights among the minor characters might seem, they serve a real purpose. They remind me of the impact of the famous *Life* magazine issue during the Vietnam War. The magazine featured the photos of every American who had died in the war during the given week—242 of them from May 28 to June 3, 1967.[2] The faces stared at you, some of them from the pages of high school yearbooks. In fact, the effect of page after page of photos, all smiling and confident, was rather like the effect of a yearbook.

That issue of *Life* was credited with personalizing the loss in Vietnam as nothing ever had before. Now, in the midst of the Iraq War, our local paper publishes a regular column featuring stories of some of those on "the roll of honor." The *Life* issue, however, had only the names and photos with excerpts from their letters, but it was the first to publish photos like this, and it had more than two hundred.

I think the effect of Homer's combat scenes, with their prefatory statements of identity, is much the same. They remind us that even the common soldier will be mourned in the village he named, by the father he revered. War is given a face from which we cannot avert our eyes. Again the war is a metaphor for the struggle of life, and here Homer shows his respect for the human struggle.

He shows little respect for the gods, who behave like the worst of men and who can do so without consequence. Granted, Zeus might singe someone's godly bottom if he was too impertinent to the chief god, and if he wanted to fight like a human he might get a wound and bleed some godly fluid. However, he would not bleed human blood and he will not die as humans must. The gods do not deserve as much respect as humans do, because the gods do not suffer consequences for their acts of foolishness or daring. Only people do.

Establishing the identities of even minor combatants has a larger significance that directly affects young people. As in *Song of Solomon*, there is very much to be found in a name. A name has to be earned, it has to establish that one is worthy of honor, it is even one's ticket to immortality. What survives of the people of *The Iliad* are their names and the stories connected to them. As in *The Odyssey*, those stories are about choice.

Even when the gods intervene, there are still choices to be made. Most of those decisions are about how and when and why one decides to join the fight, and the battle is the human battle of life. The issues are most often framed within the context of personal relationships, and the issue that dominates is one central to social order then and now: to what extent may we celebrate actions that proclaim our uniqueness, and to what extent must we curtail those actions in the interest of the greater good?

The opening lines tell us that this is the story of the wrath of Achilles. Achilles, thanks to his mother's dipping him in the river, is invulnerable except for the heel she held—the heel that holds the famous tendon with which every high school athlete is familiar. But Achilles is still offered a choice: to stay at home and live in obscurity or to die before the walls of Troy and live on in legend. When Odysseus visits with him in Hades, he seems to be having second thoughts, but his choice of the latter course is nonetheless real.

It is also his choice to withdraw in a snit from the fighting, a choice that dooms many of his fellow Greeks, but it is a human's choice, not a god's command.

Agamemnon is not Achilles' king, but he is his general, declared the first among equals by his fellow Greeks. He represents authority. When he loses his girl and demands Achilles', he is not nice about it. His decision to give a public dressing-down to his best warrior is probably ill advised. Authority figures are human too, and they do not always act with wisdom. Our reaction to this, and the reaction of any high school student, is to chafe under the unfairness of it all, under the forced submission. What should Achilles do? He quits the game, taking his football with him, and leaves the others to make do.

What they do is die in droves as the Trojans take advantage of Achilles' absence. When appeals are made to him, he becomes self-righteous. Agamemnon should not have done what he did, or at the very least should not have done it the way he did.

And what lesson does this offer for today's students? The dean of students should not have taken my iPod in front of my girlfriend. It's a stupid rule anyway, and that old fool didn't have to humiliate me. Should I punch him and go to jail? Should I stew all day and not study for any of my tests? Should I blow off tonight's game against our arch rival? Teenagers need to see that if the reaction does not fit the slight, we could make a point, but at what cost to ourselves and others? We must act with those great Greek values. We must act with reason and moderation.

This is not easy to do in emotionally charged situations, and *The Iliad* is full of such situations. Achilles ignores the consequences of his disproportionate anger, until the death of his friend Patroclus. Patroclus makes a fatal error. Once again, it is about choice. With the Trojans firing the Greek ships—their lifeline to home—he appeals to his friend to borrow his armor. In the Bible, David is offered the armor of the king of Israel, but he fights Goliath in his shepherd's clothes. He doesn't wear a king's armor—he earns the right to be king. In *The Iliad*, however, Patroclus asks for the armor, the outer trappings of the great man.

Achilles reluctantly assents, but warns him that he should only chase the Trojans from the ships and not go farther. In the heat of battle, the Trojans see what looks like Achilles and they run away. Patroclus, not satisfied with the victory, decides to ignore his friend's warning and fights to the walls of Troy, where he is killed. Patroclus's identity catches up with him. His fate is to die, but it is also his choice. Remember what nearly happened to Huck Finn when he decided to suspend his hard-fought battle for identity and put on Buck's clothes?

Patroclus's fate was to be born a lesser fighter than his friend, just as teenagers may have been born without enough height to play basketball as well as one friend or without as much ability to learn foreign languages as another. Faced with the limitations of birth, Patroclus is not the last person to try to wear somebody else's armor, somebody else's opinions, values, preferences, priorities. Ultimately, the armor will not shield us from who we are, with our own different abilities.

Faced as we all are by the limitations of our birth, we still have choices to make. Patroclus puts himself at risk to save the Greek ships. However, he is not content with this and he tempts his fate, by trying to do what only an Achilles—not a suit of Achilles' armor—can do.

Of course, Achilles cannot win the Trojan War either, though we will not learn this in *The Iliad*. The war book will end without our finding out who wins or of the sad fates that await the victors as well as the vanquished. This is not the subject of Homer's poem. The focus is on the object lesson posed by Achilles' wrath. What remains is to show Hector's choice to fight, and Achilles' choice to restore order by ultimately reining in his intemperate impulses.

There is a humanity in Hector that is missing from Achilles. This has to be so because we get to see Hector's interaction with his family, his mother and father, his siblings, his wife and child. He confronts his brother for failing to fight in the war Paris started. He bids the tenderest of farewells to his wife. He knowingly sacrifices himself for his people.

Hector knows he cannot defeat Achilles. As powerful a warrior as Hector is, this is still a David versus Goliath, with no friendly God on his side. When he realizes that the gods have deserted him, Hector can be forgiven for trying to escape. Achilles makes no bones about how this is not only a fight to the death, but how when he is done killing him, he is going to dishonor his body in front of all of Troy. Hector's family is watching from the walls.

When he has been chased around the city, Hector finally turns to face Achilles in what he knows are his final moments. He does not ask the gods to let him off the hook. He only asks that he be allowed to do something before he dies, some great deed even in defeat, which will be sung by men hereafter.

That prayer is the essence of true heroism and correct pride. We all seek a result. We want to believe that we are here for a reason, that we do not struggle aimlessly, that we will leave some mark, some footprint on life before we leave it. Teenagers may seem too convinced of their immortality to think of this too much, but they certainly think of how they can be more than one of the faceless throng. How can we distinguish ourselves? How can we at least be noticed for something?

Hector cannot live forever. He cannot even win. His defeat cannot even guarantee the safety of his family and friends. What a thoroughgoing loss this is. And yet, his prayer is answered. When we read this book, we are sitting in a classroom on the other side of the world from Troy, thousands of years later, and Hector is still with us. Even his family is still with us. We do not know the names of other heroes' wives, but we know Andromache. Hector's bravery saved her as well, saved them both from the dust of eternity, from the insignificance. This is the power of choice, of bravery, of storytelling.[3]

To the Greeks, who did not believe in heavenly reward or reincarnation, this was immortality. It is an immortality based on human choice itself rather than on divine reward. In this sense, it is not hubris. Hector has not tried to ignore the reality of his particular humanity. The gods have made him just exactly what he is. He cannot ask for more—or less. He can only ask—pray—for a chance to do something with what he was born with.

Hector makes a name for himself by doing the best he can within his fate. Hector establishes his identity for all time because he embraces his fate and balances his individualism with his duty to gods and men. Achilles, however, is bound and determined not to give in to anyone. His individual anger over the death of Patroclus literally knows no bounds. His savagery toward Hector's body and his decking Patroclus's funeral pyre with Trojan prisoners are again a refusal to acknowledge proportion.

The niceties of Greek burial customs might not be very relevant to us, but what is keenly relevant is this: while some assertion of our individuality is necessary to have an identity, some acceptance of the need to curb our individuality is necessary to have a society. Neither Agamemnon's slight nor Patroclus's death gives Achilles a right to ignore forever either his fate or his responsibility. He is a man—and part of humankind. He will eventually have to act like one.

Ironically, Achilles will relent to Priam's request for Hector's body when he is reminded of an emotional attachment. He is reminded of how his own father will grieve at the news of his death, a death he has been told will follow soon after Hector's.

Achilles had not overcome his unseemly wrath when he rejoined the battle. He simply became more furious at Hector than he had ever been at Agamemnon. Here, however, we see a more balanced man. Achilles had already seen through much of the warrior code—the very code that had required Hector's sacrifice and immortalized Hector's bravery. Ironically, it is the greatest of all the warriors who sees the limitations of this code when he tells Odysseus that the hero has no more glory than the coward.[4] Death is the verdict for both men. Ask Camus.

The Iliad, the greatest of war books, ends with the greatest of all antiwar images. The book ends without telling us who wins. It ends with both camps in mourning for a war that seems to be its own all-consuming justification, regardless of the rightness or wrongness of the cause. How similar is the constant warfare in today's Middle East? How far have we come from that ancient city in Turkey?

We have come a long way since our first consideration of Homer and the rite of passage the students were undertaking. Now it is time for them to consider what they are taking into the world and what they hope to achieve in it. All the Greeks have learned a lesson in moderation and selflessness. In the funeral games, when a victory is contested, two prizes are given. Even as the soldiers vie for glory, nothing is allowed to undermine the dignity of the event, the bonds of decency that must bind the Greeks, even as they prepare again for the warfare that is their life.

Perhaps all of the lessons learned in the books discussed in this book, all of the disparate human voices that have spoken to us through time and distance, have really been variations on this theme. A look around the average high school or a look at the average newspaper leaves us wondering at how well the rest of us have learned the lesson.

NOTES

1. Homer, *The Iliad* (W. H. D. Rouse, trans.). New York: Signet Classics, 2007.

2. "The Faces of the Dead in Vietnam—One Week's Toll." *Life*, June 27, 1967.

3. For a brilliant example of the power of story to keep people—even the storyteller—alive, read Tim O'Brien's "The Lives of the Dead," in *The Things They Carried*.

4. David Denby, "Does Homer Have Legs?" *The New Yorker*, September 6, 1993.

Chapter Sixteen

Final Thoughts

THE BOOKS I HAVE discussed are the ones I still teach every year to my eleventh and twelfth graders. I find something new in them every year, often in a student's reaction or question. Teaching high school for twenty-seven years has taught me that our maligned modern teenagers can be taught to understand, and even to love, books like these, and that once they learn this they will be better prepared for life.

Teacher and novelist Zadie Smith, in her 2003 Orange Word Lecture on E. M. Forster,[1] describes a student's brush with a great book:

> E. M. Forster's *A Room with a View* was my first intimation of the possibilities of fiction: how wholly one might feel for it and through it, how much it could do to you. I felt it was very good, and that the reading of it had done me some good. I loved it. I was too young, at 11, to realize serious people don't speak of novels this way.

Smith's "serious people" were literary critics, but who today is more serious than the educational theorist, the curriculum specialist, the deviser of assessments? One cannot be serious if one believes that students cannot read, will not work, cannot attend to anything for more than ten minutes, or will not attend to anything more challenging than that geared toward a ten-year-old.

To be fair, the literacy crisis is indeed serious and needs dedicated work for its solution. However, if we abandon the study of real literature in our schools, we jeopardize not only a generation's literacy but also its creative imagination, its vision of the past and for the future. Great books are written out of the author's compulsion to pass something along to fellow human beings about our shared condition. That message can still be made real for today's students and they will continue to respond to it if they are given the chance.

Did ever students need to hear those voices more than today? Later in her speech, Smith mentions Keats's famous "negative capability." In our information age, awash in facts, in our age of fundamentalism and victimization, ever in search for the neat answer and the easy culprit, we might be comforted to hear that "man is capable of being in uncertainties, mysteries, doubts, without any irritable reaching after fact and reason."

On the evening of the death of Martin Luther King, Jr., Robert F. Kennedy broke the news to a crowd in Indianapolis. Across the nation, cities were burning, as people sought some outlet for their rage at the murder of the man of nonviolence. Kennedy, himself only months away from an assassin's bullet, recited from memory, a passage from Aeschylus's *Agamemnon*:

> And even in our sleep
> Pain that will not forget
> falls drop by drop upon the heart
> and in our own despair
> against our will
> comes wisdom to us
> through the awful grace of god.

No speechwriter handed Kennedy this text (film of the event is easily retrievable online[2]) nor did the quote offer facile comfort. Kennedy reached back through the centuries to find poignant expression of the pain of human existence, and of the road that pain forms to something passing for human wisdom. There were no riots in Indianapolis that night.

As I end my class in June, I again pass around that ancient Greek coin and ask the students to think of their connection to all the people who have been touched by the literature we have read together, starting and ending with that blind Greek bard, himself (or herself) an image, a literary creation.

The last poem we study is Whitman's "A Noiseless, Patient Spider."[3] We began the year with Frost's "Design" and its chilling suggestion that a design of darkness to appall might be found in the spider and the flower. The spider in Whitman's poem, however, stands alone, high above the ground on some frightening edge, sending out of itself that first strand of silk that must anchor its web. It is a hero of unacknowledged effort:

> to explore the vacant, vast, surrounding,
> It launched forth filament, filament, filament, out of itself.

Adrift in the vacant, vast surrounding we have bequeathed to them, our students are launching forth those filaments, in an often frustrating attempt to anchor to something. What greater aim of education can there be than to encourage them in their effort? What better way to produce real citizens than to contribute to their success? What a tragedy, what a "throwing away of the good," it would be if we failed to realize that literature can help them craft those filaments as little else can. It can also assure them that while Whitman's spider stands "isolated" on a "little promontory," they at least are not alone.

I first heard Whitman's poem forty years ago, when another teacher, Dame Helen Gardner, used it to conclude a historic lecture series on Shakespeare. Seated as we had been for weeks, in rows of lecture hall seats, not in learning circles or cooperative groups, with not a single piece of paper in front of us but those on which we took notes, and with nothing on the wall but a clock no one looked at, there was a palpable intake of breath from the class, as she left us with the poem that has never left me:

> And you O my soul where you stand,
> Surrounded, detached, in measureless oceans of space,
> Ceaselessly musing, venturing, throwing, seeking the spheres to
> connect them,
> Till the bridge you will need be form'd, till the ductile anchor
> hold,
> Till the gossamer thread you fling catch somewhere, O my soul.

NOTES

1. Zadie Smith, "Love, Actually," *The Guardian*. November 1, 2003.

2. "Aeschylus Quotation." Retrieved from http://www.jfklibrary.org/ Historical+Resources/Archives/Reference+Desk/Speeches/RFK/Stateme nt+on+the+Assassination+of+Martin+Luther+King.htm. This is apparently a misquote from Edith Hamilton's translation, though rhetoricians have argued that his replacing "despite" with "despair" made the quote more powerful and may have been intentional.

3. Walt Whitman, "A Noiseless Patient Spider," *The Oxford Book of American Verse*. New York: Oxford University Press, 1950.

About the Author

WITH DEGREES in English literature from Fordham University and the University of Oxford, **John MacLean** has been a mill hand, merchant seaman, church sacristan, and assistant district attorney, all of which have helped him teach high school English for twenty-eight years. He and his wife, Mary, have raised four daughters.

CPSIA information can be obtained at www.ICGtesting.com
260173BV00001B/8/P

9 781607 097785